TRUE CRIME

TRUE CRIME

Nick Yapp

Bath • New York • Singapore • Hong Kong • Cologne • Delhi
Melbourne • Amsterdam • Johannesburg • Auckland • Shenzhen

This edition published by Parragon in 2011

Parragon
Queen Street House
4 Queen Street
Bath BA1 1HE, UK

ISBN 978-1-4454-3508-4

endeavour
ENDEAVOUR LONDON LTD
info@endeavourlondon.com

Text by Nick Yapp
Designer Tea Aganovic
Picture researchers Ali Khoja, Jennifer Jeffrey
Editor Mark Fletcher
Proofreader Liz Ihre

Printed in China

Frontispiece:
The bars could belong to almost any "Death Row" in an American prison. The hands are those of Michael J. Bell,
awaiting execution in Colorado State Penitentiary in 1962.

Contents

Introduction

The police "photofit" picture of the man they were seeking in connection with the Yorkshire Ripper killings. It was published in 1979, a year in which Sutcliffe was twice interviewed by the police. It took another two years and three more killings before Sutcliffe was arrested and charged.

The vast majority of criminals pass quickly through the justice system, receive their punishments and disappear into obscurity. A few become famous. Often this is because the crimes they have committed are so bestial or so heinous that the law-abiding world cannot forget them. That is how Bluebeard and the Vampire of Düsseldorf achieved their places in history. Others gain notoriety through their choice of victim. Few people today would know of John Wilkes Booth had he not gone to the theatre one night and shot the President of the United States, indeed, many killers have chosen assassination as their particular crime simply as a means of achieving fame. Some 80 years down the line, the name Bruno Hauptmann is still reviled because he was found guilty of the kidnapping and murder of an innocent child, the infant son of a great American hero.

And many criminals are remembered for other reasons. Eugene Weidmann's unhappy claim to fame is that he was the last person to be publicly guillotined in France. Ruth Ellis is remembered because she was the last woman to be executed in Britain – had she killed her lover in France she might still be alive today, for hers was indisputably a *crime passionnel*. Half a century after the Great Train Robbery, Ronald Biggs is remembered as much for his prison escape as for the crime itself; Doctor Crippen's crime might well have been forgotten had it not been for the manner of his arrest. The most notorious – killers such as Charles Manson, Jack the Ripper, Al Capone – have gone down in history because for a couple of weeks, a few months, or a lifetime, their evil deeds held the world spellbound in fear and horror.

Men like these, and the few women that have matched them, rarely appeal for any attractive reasons, although some have passed into legend in the manner of Robin Hood or Till Eulenspiegel, snapping their fingers at society, living a devil-may-care existence and luring the public into being momentarily on their side. Plenty of Americans were thrilled when Bonnie and Clyde or John Dillinger eluded lawmen, and some were even saddened when these desperadoes were gunned down in a hail of bullets. To the public, it was as though a great adventure story had come to a sudden end.

In general, however, the names of the killers and robbers, kidnappers and gangsters that have left a trail of corpses on the high road of history live on only in infamy. Here is a photographic record of what these people did, a rogues' gallery of the culprits, and some brief attempts to suggest what prompted them to break the best known of the Ten Commandments.

Outlaws and Anarchists

Armed cattle rustlers cut wire fences on the Brighton
Ranch in Custer County, Nebraska, in 1885.

The myths and legends of the Wild West have been well served and well plundered by films, books and songs. The same cannot be said for the truth. In a world where the Rule of Law had at best a precarious hold on society, the line between "lawman" and "desperado" was blurred. Men like Wyatt Earp, Wild Bill Hickock, and even Bat Masterson had days when they were gunslingers and law enforcers at one and the same time. Out of this confusion, it was popular opinion of the time that decided whether a robber, an outlaw, or a gunslinger was hero or villain, and back in the 1870s, 1880s and 1890s, popular opinion decided that Jesse James was most definitely a hero.

James had the good luck to be championed by the press, in particular by John Newman Edwards, then editor of the *Kansas City Times*, and a man who campaigned for the return to power of old Confederate supporters in the state of Missouri. In a society of predominately small farmers, who loathed the banks that the James–Younger gang stole from, and had little sympathy for "Yankee" railroad companies and detective agencies it took only rumours of good deeds on the part of outlaws to turn Jesse James and his like into Robin Hood figures, stealing from the rich to give to the poor. In the case of Jesse, the legend was completed by the manner of his death – shot in the back by Bob Ford, a treacherous member of his own gang, greedy for the reward offered for "Jesse James, Dead or Alive".

William H. Bonney, aka William Henry McCarty but better known as Billy the Kid, was never so lucky. His was a sad and messy life, serving no popular cause, righting no wrongs and doing little to help his fellow poor – not the stuff of which heroes are made. He was orphaned at the age of 13 and placed in a foster home by his stepfather. He fell in with a small-time crook named Sombrero Jack, and first fell foul of the law by stealing laundry. He spent the next two

The Wild West

The "Dirty little coward, who shot Mr. Howard": Bob Ford displays the gun with which he shot Jesse James.

years tramping the country and working as a ranch hand and professional gambler, before teaming up with a horse thief named Jack Mackie. Most of Billy's companions were themselves pathetic creatures and unsuccessful criminals. Serious trouble came when he was 16. Billy shot and killed Frank "Windy" Cahill, a bully who picked on him once too often. Billy fled to New Mexico where he teamed up with Jesse Evans and his gang of rustlers known as "The Boys".

Unlike Jesse James, whose exploits were praised by the press, the teenage Billy the Kid and "The Boys" were denounced by Colonel Albert Fountain, editor of his local

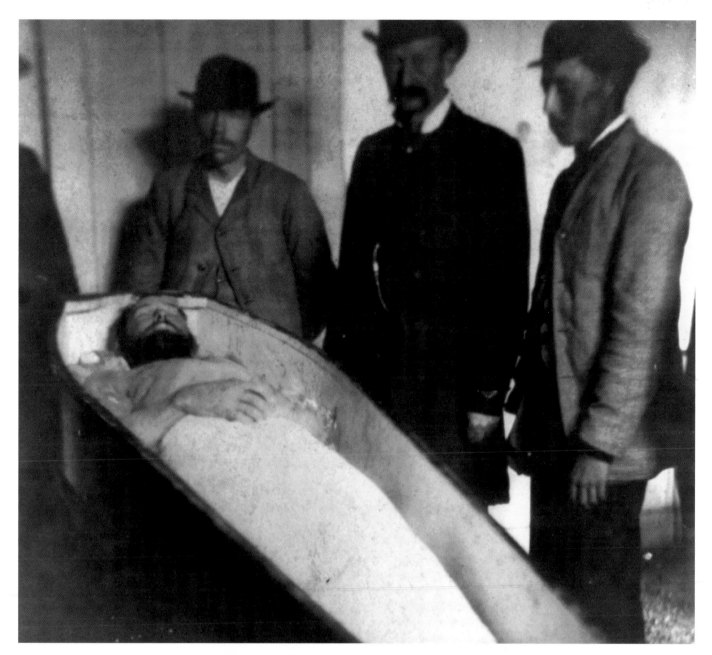

(*top left*) A "WANTED" poster for Billy the Kid, issued c.1878. (*top middle*) William "Billy the Kid" Bonney at the age of 21, with just a year of his life left. (*above*) Frank James (standing centre) stands over the coffin of his brother Jesse, Sidenfaden Funeral Parlor, St. Joseph, Missouri, April 4, 1882. (*left*) A portrait of Frank James, dating from 1863. (*middle*) Jesse James, a year after his first killing in the raid on a bank in Gallatin, Missouri. (*far left*) Pat Garrett, the sheriff who tracked down and killed Billy the Kid.

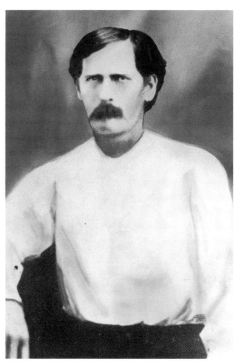

14

REMAINS OF M°LAURY = EAR

Mesilla Valley Independent. Billy was repeatedly let down by life: deserted by his father, spurned by his stepfather and bullied by the first man he killed. He was betrayed by the Governor of New Mexico – Lew Wallace, author of Ben Hur – who had promised Billy exemption from prosecution following violence and murder in a power struggle between rival "rings" in Lincoln County and finally killed by the man he had befriended and trusted, Sheriff Pat Garrett.

(clockwise from top of page) The Wild Bunch, c.1885: (left to right) Harry Langbaugh (The Sundance Kid), William Carver, Ben Kilpatrick, Harvey Logan, and Butch Cassidy Parker. Three members of the Clanton Gang shot by Wyatt Earp and his posse at the OK Corral: (left to right) Tom McLaury, Frank McLaury, and Billy Clanton. Wild Bill Hickock, cowboy, scout, gambler, gunfighter, and part-time lawman. William "Bat" Masterson with the cane he carried all his life, following a wound received in his first gunfight. Wyatt Earp in his mid-twenties.

In the 100 years that had passed since Mexico had overthrown Spanish rule, there had been a succession of wars, coups, and power struggles, but by 1910 Mexico had experienced over 30 years of stability under its strong-arm president, Porfirio Diaz. That was about to come to an end. In the election of 1910, Diaz declared himself the winner by an almost unanimous vote. It was a blatant fraud, which the people did not accept. Riots broke out. Armed insurrection began, and among the many who took up arms were Emilio Zapata ("The Tiger") and José Doroteo Arango Arambula ("The Centaur", better known as Pancho Villa). Both men were champions of the poor – the *peones* and the *campesinos*. Both had a natural genius for the art of warfare. Both achieved lasting fame, becoming the heroes of many books, films and songs. And both men were to die by assassination.

They were almost exact contemporaries, but came from very different backgrounds. Zapata was the son of an independent *ranchero*, a man never in danger of poverty. Villa, on the other hand, was a poor sharecropper. Zapata had already spent time campaigning for the rights of villagers and the redistribution of land under the slogan "*Tierra y libertad*" ("Land and freedom"). Villa was an outlaw, a man who had become a bandit and cattle rustler after shooting the owner of a *hacienda*, who had raped Villa's young sister.

When the revolution broke out, both men placed themselves in the service of Francisco Madero, one of several candidates for the Mexican presidency. They had immediate success, most famously Villa's victory at the first Battle of Juarez, where his Army of the North inflicted a crushing defeat on the conscript armies of Diaz. Significantly, in the light of what was to come, there was a US presence at the battle, a group of Americans viewing the fighting from the top of railroad boxcars in El Paso.

Emilio Zapata & Pancho Villa

At the height of their fame, Emilio Zapata (*left*) and Pancho Villa sit in adjacent thrones, January 2, 1915.

SILLA PRESIDENCIAL CASASOLA No 6.

Madero became President, but not for long. In his service was General Victoriano Huerta, a man already conspiring with Felix Diaz (son of the ex-President) and US ambassador Henry Lane Wilson to make himself dictator of Mexico. Huerta crushed a rebellion against Madero, but in 1913 proclaimed himself President, ordered the assassination of Madero, and put an end to all land reforms. Zapata and Villa now took up the cause of another presidential candidate, Venustiano Carranza.

This was the beginning of the golden age of Zapata and Villa. Widely acclaimed as champions of the poor, and with the ranks of their separate armies swelled with angry peasants, their exploits were celebrated at home and abroad. It

(*top*) Pancho Villa, on the white horse, and his followers, c.1914. (*left*) Emilio Zapata at the time of the agrarian uprising in South Mexico, 1913. (*right*) A street execution carried out by followers of Venustiano Carranza, 1915.

was the last summer of the age of cavalry. Mounted on fine horses, the well-armed *bandolieros* achieved the status of latter-day Robin Hoods, stealing from the rich to give to the poor. Woodrow Wilson, newly elected President of the United States, dismissed Ambassador Wilson, and took up the cause of Carranza, halting the supply of foreign arms and ammunition to Huerta by blockading the port of Vera Cruz. While Zapata controlled the south, Villa won a series of battles at Ciudad Juarez, Tierra Blanca, Chihuahua, and Ojinaga. In December 1914 Zapata and Villa met for the first time and made their historic entry into Mexico City. The following year, Carranza was recognized as President of Mexico by the United States and several Latin American countries. Huerta left Mexico and went into exile on July 14, 1914.

Out of success came splits and recriminations between Carranza and his two great generals. For a while Wilson continued to support Villa, but the *Villistas* suffered defeats. In 1916 Villa led his men into New Mexico, attacking the town of Columbus and killing 10 American soldiers and eight civilians. With Carranza's approval, Wilson sent an army of 11,000 men under General Pershing across the border into Mexico to hunt down Villa. They never succeeded in finding him and the U.S. troops were withdrawn in 1917 when they were needed on the battlefields of Europe.

Zapata survived another five years before being lured into an ambush by Colonel Jesus Guajardo. The Colonel had intimated that he wished to join Zapata's revolutionaries, but when Zapata arrived at the meeting place, he was gunned down. Villa went into semi-retirement and survived until 1923, when he was assassinated while sitting in his car in Parral, Chihuahua.

American intervention... (*top*) General John Pershing leads his cavalry in pursuit of Pancho Villa, 1916. (*above*) The U.S. Navy prepares to bombard Vera Cruz, 1914. (*opposite*) The Stars and Stripes flies over the Terminal Hotel, Vera Cruz, headquarters of Rear Admiral Frank Fletcher during the Mexican Civil War, 1914.

In the early years of the 20th century, the Liberal government in Britain, of which a young Winston Churchill was Home Secretary, came under much criticism for its lenient immigration policy, which allowed a great many political and economic refugees from Russia and the Balkan States into London. A gang of Latvian anarchists under the leadership of Peter Piaktow – popularly known as Peter the Painter – embarked on a series of crimes, which included the killing of four policemen in Houndsditch. In the massive hunt for those responsible that followed these murders, several of the gang were captured. On New Year's Day 1911, an informant told police that other members of the gang were holed up at 100 Sidney Street. By 2.00 am on January 3, 200 police had cordoned off the street and surrounded the house.

The gang were better armed than the police, and a call went out for a company of Scots Guards to be deployed from the Tower of London. News of this reached Churchill, who leapt from his bath, dressed and hurried to Sidney Street. He was greeted with taunts from the large crowd that had gathered to watch the battle. "Who let 'em in?" was the cry. Churchill is said to have had no wish to assume personal command, although he was profligate with advice – that heavy artillery should be brought up to shell the house and that police and troops should storm the property, carrying before them a steel shield. Neither idea was adopted, for suddenly smoke was seen pouring from an upstairs window. The fire brigade arrived, but Churchill refused to allow them access. Within a short time the upper floors collapsed and when police were eventually able to enter the building, they found the charred remains of two of the gang, Fritz Svaars and William Sokolow. There was no sign of Peter the Painter.

Over the next few weeks Churchill was repeatedly jeered at for the part he had played in the strange battle. Five members of the gang were later put on trial, but the prosecution of the case was poorly handled and all were acquitted.

Sidney Street Siege

Crowds gather as a company of Scots Guards keep watch on Sidney Street, January 3, 1911. Armed troops had not been seen on London streets since Bloody Sunday in 1887. (*inset*) A young Winston Churchill.

John Dillinger was a good-looking guy, a ladies' man with a smile not unlike that of Frank Sinatra. Unlike Frank, however, Dillinger neither drank nor smoked, and claimed that his one bad habit was robbing banks – a habit he picked up late in his short life. He was the archetypal American gangster of the 1930s – fearless, ruthless, always with a broad on one arm and a Tommy-gun tucked under the other.

Although he had been a rebellious youth, it was not until he deserted from the U.S. Navy that Dillinger turned to crime. In September 1924 he stole $555 from a local grocer in his hometown of Mooresville. He was arrested, convicted, and sent to Michigan City State Prison for the next eight years. He was released on parole in May 1933 and spent the rest of his life on the run. The desperate spree began when Dillinger and two ex-cons named John Hamilton and Harry Pierpont robbed a number of banks in Indiana and Ohio. Dillinger was caught, but Hamilton and Pierpont broke into the jail where he was held and freed him. The three men then broke into two Indiana police stations to obtain fresh supplies of guns and bullet-proof vests.

For three months the robberies continued, but big trouble started in January 1934 when Dillinger killed a policeman during a bank raid in East Chicago. He had hit the big time. The posters were up all over the States. Dillinger was Public Enemy Number One. He was recognized and arrested in Tucson, Arizona, and given a 20-year sentence. Just two weeks later, however, he escaped from jail, forcing the guards to back off by brandishing a wooden pistol he had hand-carved and smeared with boot polish.

He tried to disguise his good looks, growing a moustache and having a face lift. He also bathed his fingertips in acid to destroy his fingerprints. The raiding and the killing continued. Acting on a

John Dillinger

"Public Enemy Number One" – the notorious killer and bank robber John Dillinger, a photograph taken when he was on the run.

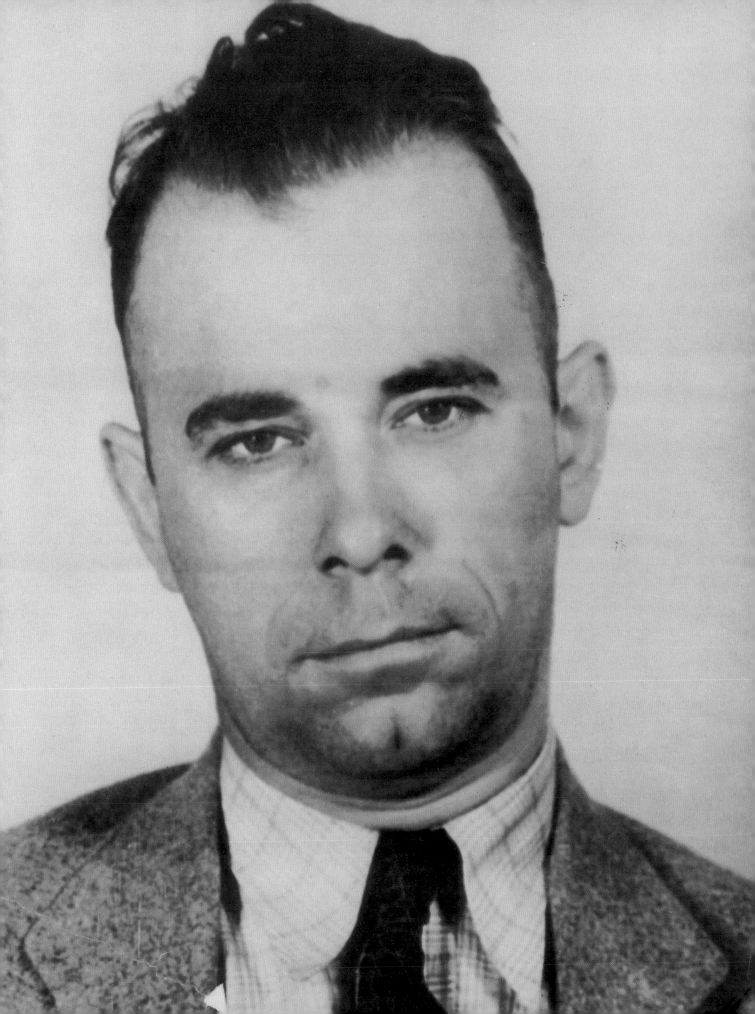

tip from the wife of Dillinger's landlord, on March 31, 1934, the police in St. Paul, Minnesota, set up an ambush, but Dillinger and two accomplices managed to shoot their way out. On April 23 Dillinger escaped two more posses, killing two policemen and wounding five others. The end was very near.

Chicago police persuaded a prostitute named Anna Sage to befriend Dillinger. On the night of July 22, 1934, Dillinger and Sage went to a movie theatre to see Clark Gable play the part of a gangster in a film called *Manhattan Melodrama*. Sage wore a bright red dress, so that she would be clearly recognized by the police waiting outside. As Dillinger came out, one of the cops called his name – "John!" Dillinger turned and was gunned down in a hail of bullets. At the time, he was wanted for 16 murders.

(*clockwise from above*) An unhappy eight-year-old Dillinger on his father's Indiana farm. A Boy Scout truck in Dillinger country, Wisconsin, at a time when police and law agents were as trigger-happy as the gunmen they pursued, April 26, 1934. Dillinger is handcuffed to Deputy Police Chief Carroll Holby, with defense attorney Joseph Ryan on Dillinger's left, Crown Point, Indiana, February 5, 1934. The FBI poster on Dillinger in June 1934, a month before he was gunned down by police in Chicago.

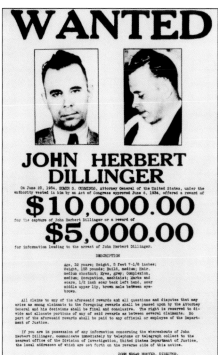

It was a bumpy ride while it lasted. Clyde Champion Barrow and Bonnie Parker first met in January 1930. Just over four years later they died in an early morning hail of bullets from police and Texas Rangers on a highway near Sailes, Louisiana. In those intervening four years, they had killed 13 people, committed a series of robberies, and assisted in a couple of jail-breaks. Clyde's brother Buck died in custody after a shootout at Platte City, Missouri; his sister-in-law was blinded in the same shootout; and Bonnie was severely burnt and crippled in an automobile wreck.

They were young. When they met, Clyde was 21 and unmarried, and Bonnie was just 19, married to an imprisoned murderer. A month later, Clyde was in jail for robbery, but Bonnie smuggled a gun into him and he escaped. Recaptured almost immediately, Clyde spent the next two years in prison. He was released in February 1932 and the killing started. The first victim was a storeowner in Hillsboro, gunned down as they robbed the store. From then on, they were trigger-happy, killing anyone that got in their way. In all this mayhem, they seemed to have charmed lives, surviving at least two ambushes – one in Iowa (July 1933), another on a highway near Grand Prairie, Texas (November 1933).

That same year, however, the FBI became involved, simply because Bonnie and Clyde had been identified as responsible for the interstate transportation of two stolen automobiles. The luck of the outlaws changed. On May 22, 1934, their pursuers learned that they were due to return to Black Lake, Louisiana the following day. A third ambush was set up. Bonnie and Clyde were killed instantly. Clyde was 25. Bonnie was 23.

On the headstone of Bonnie's grave in the Crown Hill Cemetery, Dallas, the inscription reads: "As the flowers are all made sweeter by the sunshine and the dew, so this old world is made brighter by the lives of folks like you." Storeowners, the Louisiana, and Texas police and the FBI may not have agreed with the sentiment.

Bonnie and Clyde

Bonnie Parker and Clyde Barrow poke fun at death and violence in 1932. Two years later death and violence had the last laugh.

The late 1960s were heady days for extreme political activists across Europe, among them the middle-class members of the extreme New Left group in Germany called the Red Army Faction (RAF). Among its early leaders were Andreas Baader, Thorwald Proll, Horst Sohnlein, and Gudrun Ensslin. They began by plotting to set fire to several large department stores, which they saw as icons of capitalism. Ulrike Meinhof, a like-minded journalist, joined in 1968.

The authorities came down very heavily: Baader, Meinhof and others were imprisoned, kept in solitary confinement, denied the usual visiting arrangements, and were force-fed when they went on hunger strike. Meinhof committed suicide by hanging herself. All of which did little to halt the RAF's activities. Between May 1972 and October 1977, a second generation RAF was credited with over a dozen acts of terrorism. They bombed police stations, U.S. barracks, and the US Military Intelligence Headquarters in West Germany. They assassinated the Federal Prosecutor-General Siegfried Buback. They occupied the West German Embassy in Stockholm.

Their campaign of terror peaked in September and October 1977, which became known as *Der Deutsche Herbst*, the German Autumn. Hans-Martin Schleyer, President of the Association of German Industry, was kidnapped and shot by the RAF and a Lufthansa airliner was hijacked at Palma Airport, Mallorca. The West German government faced the crisis with force, refused to come to terms and eventually sent GSG9, an elite unit of the German Federal Police to storm the plane. In a remarkably successful operation all four hijackers were killed.

Baader, Ensslin, and other RAF leaders were already in prison when news of the hijack failure came through on their hidden radios. Next morning, Baader was found dead with a gunshot wound to the head, and Ensslin was found hanging in her cell. The Left suspected foul play, but it now seems likely that both deaths were suicide. On April 20, 1998, a fax to Reuters news agency announced that the group had been dissolved.

Baader Meinhof

(*top*) The arrest of Andreas Baader in Frankfurt, June 1972. Leaders of the Red Army Faction: (*left to right*) Ulrike Meinhof, Gudrun Ensslin, Jan Carl Raspe, and Andreas Baader.

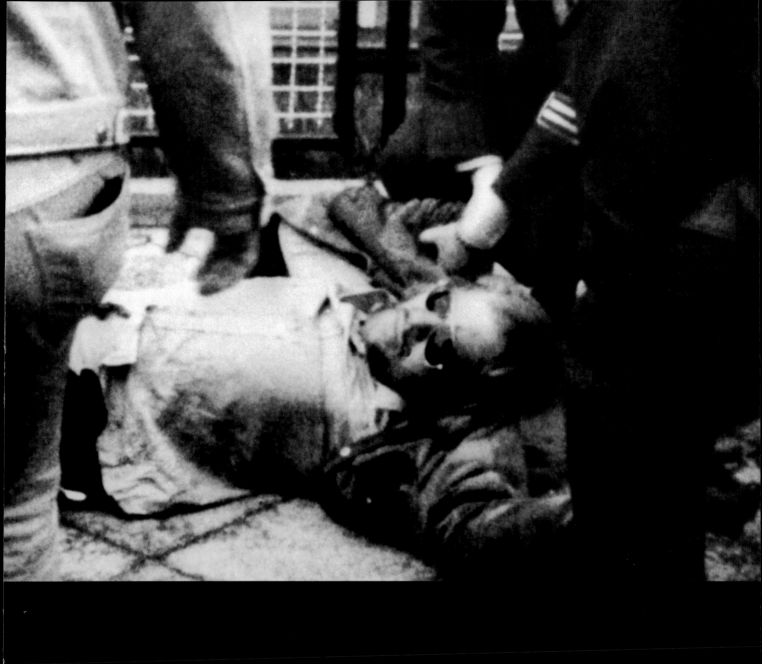

On the night of September 4, 1972, eight masked terrorists entered the Israeli quarters at the Olympic Village in Munich. They were members of the Black September Organization (BSO), dedicated to the Palestinian cause and to the overthrow of King Hussein of Jordan. Two members of the Israeli team, Yossef Gutfreund and Yossef Romano, strongly resisted the BSO terrorists, protecting other Israeli athletes and fighting back. Eventually both were killed. Nevertheless, the terrorists were able to take nine hostages.

The terrorists then made their demands – that 234 Palestinians and non-Arabs should be released from jails in Egypt and given safe passage out of that country. They also wanted the German authorities to release Andreas Baader and Ulrike Meinhof, then in jail for crimes committed by the Red Army Faction. The German authorities refused, but offered unlimited money instead. This was turned down by the terrorists, who replied "money means nothing to us, our lives mean nothing to us".

The morning of September 5 passed in unsuccessful negotiations between the terrorists and the Munich police chief and the head of the Egyptian Olympic team. Late in the day, the terrorists demanded transportation to Cairo. At 10.10 pm, two helicopters took both terrorists and hostages to the nearby Fürstenfeldbrück airbase, where two members of Mossad, German police, and five German snipers were waiting. None of the snipers was equipped with telescopic sights or night-vision scopes, and none had received special training. On the airbase runway was a Boeing 727 with a handful of armed German police inside, disguised as flight crew. The plan was that these men would deal with the terrorists from the first helicopter while the snipers took out those from the second, but at the last minute the German police on board the 727 aborted their mission.

Black September

The chilling image of one of the Black September gang members in the Olympic Village, Munich, September 7, 1972.

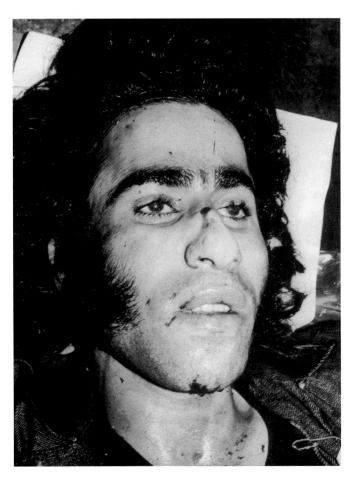

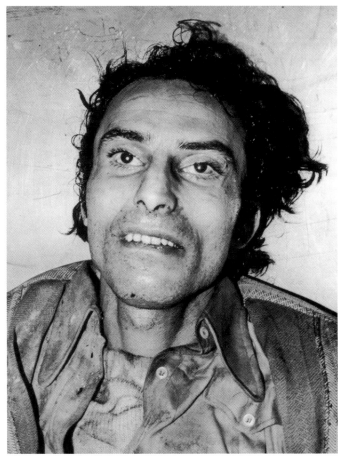

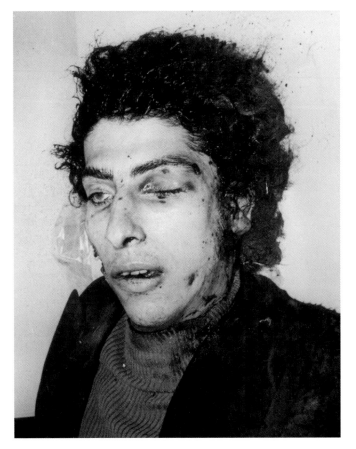

The helicopters touched down at 10.30 pm. Four of the BSO terrorists held the pilots at gunpoint. Two others boarded the 727. Finding it empty, they knew that they had been tricked and that there was no deal. Almost at once, the German authorities ordered the snipers to open fire. There was immediate chaos. Two of the terrorists were killed, but others scrambled to safety and returned fire. The helicopters' pilots fled, but the hostages were tied up and could not move from the helicopters. In the confusion German police fired on their own snipers, seriously wounding one, while others attempted to continue negotiations. At 0.06 am on September 6, the terrorists began killing their hostages. In all 17 people died – 11 members of the Israeli team, one German policeman, and five of the terrorists.

Avery Brundage, President of the International Olympic Committee, made no reference to the massacre when he later made a speech praising the strength of the Olympic movement.

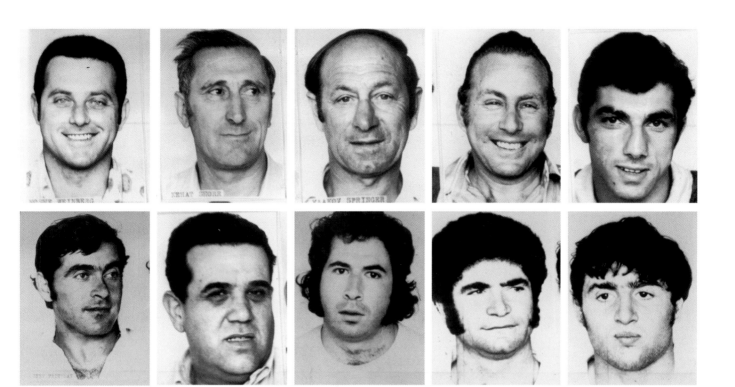

(*opposite*) Three of the Palestinian terrorists. (*above, top row, left to right*) The victims: Moshe Weinberg, Kehat Schur, Yakov Springer, Amitzur Shapira, and Eliezaar Halfen. (*bottom row, left to right*) Zeev Friedman, Yossef Gutfreund, David Berger, Yosef Romano, and Mark Slavin. (*right*) *Time* magazine cover for September 18, 1972.

FIFTY CENTS   SEPTEMBER 18, 1972

TIM

**Murder
in Munich**

Ill-gotten Gains

Arrested narcotic dealers appear at the Federal
Building in Chicago on March 1, 1954.

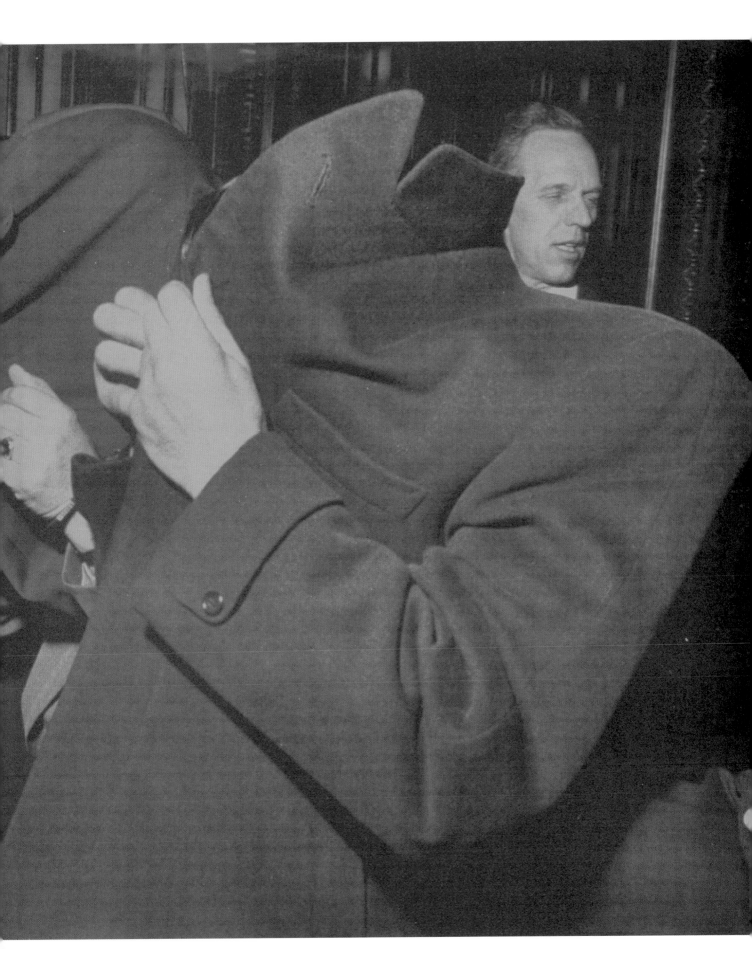

In 1854 Roger Tichborne, heir to an enormously valuable estate, embarked from Rio de Janeiro. He was never seen again. His mother, Lady Tichborne, refused to believe him dead and placed advertisements for him in the English and colonial papers. Ten years passed until Lady Tichborne learned that a man answering her beloved son's description had been found in Wagga Wagga, New South Wales. She wrote, imploring the man to return to her. A year later Arthur Orton and Lady Tichborne met in a Paris hotel one grim January afternoon. She professed to recognize him, although Roger had weighed only 11 stone and the man before her weighed 21 stone. Lady Tichborne joyfully brought Orton home to Hampshire and settled an allowance on him of £1000 per annum. She died 12 months later.

Orton's immediate problem was that he had already borrowed heavily in anticipation of grabbing the immense Tichborne fortune. Fortunately, those 12 months had given him time to acquaint himself with Roger's past and Roger's ways, as recounted to him by a black servant named Bogle. Villagers and the local gentry accepted Orton as Roger. Officers who had served with Roger in the 6th Dragoon Guards were also convinced. The family solicitor believed him to be Roger. Unfortunately, the trustees of the Tichborne estate did not. Orton was compelled to bring an action against Sir Henry Tichborne, who had been declared the legitimate heir.

The action lasted 102 days, 22 of which were taken up by the cross-examination of Orton by Sir John Coleridge. Orton lost the case and was immediately charged with perjury. His trial lasted 188 days. He was found guilty, sentenced to 14 years' penal servitude and sent to Dartmoor. Inasmuch as the truth ever emerged, it seemed that Orton had simply been an Australian stockman, slaughter-man, and part-time horse thief, with a bold sense of adventure, a cast-iron nerve and a desire for wealth.

Tichborne Claimant

Arthur Orton, the 21-stone Australian butcher who claimed to be the true twelfth baronet Sir Roger Tichborne, and heir to an immense estate.

Frau Thérèse Humbert was born in 1856, the daughter of a peasant couple in Aussonne, Languedoc. As a girl she showed a natural propensity for fraud, persuading her friends to pool their jewellery and thereby fool others, particularly young men, into believing that they were wealthy. By such means she was able to marry Frédéric Humbert, son of the mayor of Toulouse. In 1880 she took the first steps in what was to become known as the Trouser Button Fraud.

Thérèse claimed that on a train journey she had heard groans coming from the adjoining compartment. She had clambered along the outside of the coach from one compartment to the next, where she found an American millionaire named Robert Henry Crawford having a heart attack. Restored to health, the grateful Crawford promised he would reward her. In 1881 came a letter informing her that Crawford had died, leaving her a considerable sum of money. She was also to look after his wealth until her younger sister Marie was old enough to marry Crawford's nephew. That "wealth" was to be kept in a sealed safe. Armed with this story, and with the safe as collateral, the Humberts obtained a huge loan, and moved to Paris. For 20 years they lived in luxury. The original loans had to be repaid, but Frau Humbert had no difficulty in obtaining new loans to pay off the old. Eventually, the bank asked what the "wealth" consisted of. Frau Humbert replied it was in government bonds. The bank checked. There was no record of the purchase of such bonds. The French newspaper *Le Matin* demanded an investigation, and in 1902 the court ordered that the safe be opened.

Inside was a brick and an English halfpenny, although a rumour spread that it contained a trouser button. Thousands of investors were ruined. Frau Humbert fled to Madrid, was arrested, brought back to France and sentenced to five years' hard labour. On her release from prison she disappeared, and was never heard of again.

Frau Humbert

The removal of the Humberts' safe from their house.
(*inset*) Frau Thérèse Humbert, the fraudster who claimed that she was the recipient of vast sums of money from a grateful American millionaire.

The case of Serge Alexandre Stavisky was to create a financial empire on the ownership of "the emeralds of the late Empress of Germany", emeralds that turned out to be glass. Stavisky came to France from Russia after the Bolshevik revolution. At first he made a modest living as a café singer, nightclub manager and gambler, later moving to Bayonne in southwest France where he became manager of a chain of municipal pawnshops. He issued hundreds of millions of francs' worth of false bonds, claiming they would be honoured by the City of Bayonne. The bonds were bought largely by insurance companies acting, according to *The New Yorker,* on the advice of "the Minister of the Colonies, who was counselled by the Minister of Commerce, who was counselled by the Mayor of Bayonne, who was counselled by Stavisky".

Suspicion grew, and Stavisky's affairs were investigated by newspaper reporters and the police. In 1927 he was put on trial for fraud, but the trial was repeatedly postponed, and Stavisky was bailed 19 times. Finally, in December 1933, enough evidence had been obtained to expose him. He fled to Chamonix, where he is said to have committed suicide, though it was also alleged that police killed him.

In the messy aftermath, the French Prime Minister was forced to resign, the Prefect of the Paris Police was dismissed, the right-wing director of the *Comédie Française* was replaced by the left-wing Head of the *Sûreté-Générale*, and riots broke out on the streets of Paris. As many as 14 people were killed, most of them by the police.

In the subsequent trials of Stavisky's associates, all the accused were acquitted. The amount of money "lost" in the scam is said to have amounted to some $60 million in present-day values.

Stavisky Scandal

Madame Arlette Stavisky, wife of the swindler Alexandre Stavisky, as she appeared on the front cover of the French magazine *Vu* in 1933.

VU

640 MILLIONS + STAVISK... = 14 FRANC... + 1 POUP...

Mme Stavisky, u...
parisienne, quitta...
ridge quelques...
son mari pour s'i...
un appartement...

On August 8, 1963, on a quiet stretch of line in Bedfordshire, the Glasgow to London "up-postal" train was robbed of over £2.5 million. It was one of the most audacious crimes in British history. Bruce Reynolds, a London antique dealer and accomplished thief, recruited a team of 15 men for the job, including a railroad expert, a train driver and an expert electrician. He negotiated the purchase of Leatherslade Farm as a hideout 27 miles from the site of the planned robbery, and stole army uniforms, an army lorry and two Land Rovers.

The planning was meticulous, the execution faultless. Just after midnight, disguised as an army team on manoeuvres, the gang left the isolated farm and drove to Bridego Bridge. At 3:00 am, Roger Cordrey, the electrician, and another member of the gang activated false signals, bringing the mail train to a halt at Sears Crossing. The train was split and, since the gang's own driver was unable to release the vacuum brake, Jack Mills, the real train driver, was forced to shunt the locomotive and the first two coaches to Bridego Bridge, where the rest of the gang waited. The postal workers in the mail coach were gagged, bound and left lying face-down on the floor of the coach. The gang then formed a human chain down the embankment to the waiting lorry. Just forty minutes from the time the train had been stopped, Reynolds and his men made their get-away back to Leatherslade Farm.

The police responded quickly. From their radio, the gang learned that the police knew an army vehicle had been involved in the robbery and suspected that those responsible were holed up in a local farmhouse. One of the gang, Buster Edwards, suggested that they burn the farm to the ground – to avoid leaving fingerprints or other evidence. The idea was rejected. Smoke and flames in high summer might attract unwelcome attention, and, anyway, someone had been paid to "sanitize" the farmhouse the moment they left.

Great Train Robbery

An aerial photograph of the site of what was then the greatest train robbery in the history of British crime – the line from Cheddington Station to Bridego Bridge, August 1963.

That "someone" did nothing, and when police raided the farm they discovered fingerprints of everyone involved – on beer bottles, ketchup bottles and on pieces of a Monopoly set the gang had played with to while away the hours. One by one, the gang were arrested – Cordrey, Charles Wilson, James White, Thomas Wisbey, James Hussey, Robert Welch, Reynolds, Edwards, Gordon Goody, Brian Field, William Boal, Leonard Field and Ronald Biggs. All received lengthy jail sentences.

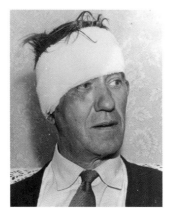

Biggs alone of the gang, achieved folk-hero status. This was largely as a result of his escape from prison on July 8, 1965, his flight to Australia and then to Brazil and his subsequent battle to stay out of the hands of the British police over a period of 37 years, before giving himself up on May 7, 2001. On August 6, 2009, Biggs was released from prison on compassionate grounds.

(*opposite top row*) Three of the robbers: James White, Charles Wilson, and Bruce Reynolds. (*opposite middle row*) Ronnie Biggs; the train driver, Jack Mills, with his head bandaged shortly after the robbery. (*opposite below*) Three of the suspects arrested in connection with the "Great Train Robbery" leaving Linslade Court with blankets over their heads on August 16, 1963. (*above*) Banknotes hidden in the walls of the caravan of James White. The police found £35,000 here.

When stock markets are manipulated by insider trading, innocent people will almost always lose money, and the money they have lost simply ceases to exist. It cannot be handed back. If a member of the public buys stock at $10 a share, and the value of that stock falls by 10 per cent, then not only has that person lost a dollar a share, that dollar has disappeared. And if the value of the stock falls by over 90 per cent, as it did in the case of the Enron Corporation, then some people may lose almost all they own.

When the crash came for Enron in December 2001, investors lost some $60 billion, the firm's accounts going back five years had to be rewritten, and Enron filed for bankruptcy. As in the fall of the Roman Empire, too many people had been having too good a time to see what was coming, which is all it takes for others to hasten and worsen the collapse by adding a little mischief of their own. Long before the courts of law had found anyone guilty in the Enron affair, the court of public opinion had tried and condemned certain parties – notably the accounting firm of Arthur Andersen. As papers were hurriedly shredded and files destroyed, one expert pronounced the last rites on Andersen: "The verdict doesn't matter any more. Arthur Andersen is dead." He was right. The giant accounting firm crashed to the ground on August 31, 2002, though the Supreme Court subsequently quashed Andersen's conviction.

In court, the top echelon of Enron cut sorry figures. Kenneth Lay, former Chair of Enron, asserted that the collapse was primarily the fault of the *Wall Street Journal* for publishing articles that had "kicked off a run on the bank". He might perhaps more justifiably have blamed one particular journalist – Bethany McLean, whose 2001 article in the ironically-named magazine *Fortune* first suggested that the company was overvalued. It was her persistence that ultimately led to the "smartest guys in the room" looking so silly in court. Lay died of a heart attack on July 5, 2006 three months before his scheduled sentencing.

Enron

(*top left*) Enron Headquarters in downton Houston, Texas, August 13, 1999. "The Smartest Guys in the Room": (*top right*) Andrew Fastow, former Chief Financial Officer; (*bottom left*) Ken Lay, former CEO; and (bottom right) David B. Duncan, former Arthur Andersen accountant.

1400 Smith Street

When Nick Leeson's rogue trading made $15 million for Barings Bank, few questions were asked as to how it was done. They never are, for a kind of magic attaches to the process. All that changes is the sum of money involved. Leeson cost Barings $1.4 billion and destroyed the bank; Jérôme Kerviel cost the Société Générale $7 billion and brought it to the brink of collapse.

Kerviel was born in 1977, the son of a Breton blacksmith and a hairdresser. At university, he was a diligent but not outstanding student. On graduation, he immediately joined the SocGen and in 2005 became a junior trader in the bank's Delta One division in Paris. In 2006, he was awarded a $70,000 bonus on top his $80,000 salary. It wasn't enough. Kerviel wanted 10 times as much the following year, and began pursuing that amount by engaging in allegedly unauthorized trading to the value of some $50 billion.

For a time, the profits rolled in, and Kerviel gained the nickname *le cash machine*. "I was taking crazy risks," he said. "It's a bit like playing a video game. Losing or winning millions, it only takes a few seconds." His actions were highly secretive, however, and dangerously speculative. When the SocGen discovered what was going on, they hastily shut down Kerviel's operation, but it was too late. The market in which Kerviel had been dealing collapsed, and the SocGen lost almost $6 billion in three days.

Unlike Leeson, Kerviel did not flee. He stayed to face his accusers, and to counter-claim through his lawyers that the bank's managers had "brought the loss on themselves". Sceptics find it impossible to believe that SocGen was ignorant of what was going on. Kerviel was arrested, formally charged with abuse of confidence and illegal access to computers. In October 2010, Kerviel was found guilty and sentenced to five years' imprisonment, with two years suspended. He was also told to pay damages to SocGen of €4.9 billion – the sum of money his risky betting strategies cost his former employers in 2008. Kerviel's lawyer said that his client would appeal.

Jérôme Kerviel

Jérôme Kerviel is released on bail from La Santé Prison by a Parisian court on March 18, 2008 in Paris, France.

All good conmen know that the secret of success is to appear reluctant to admit victims to the scam they are running. Bernie Madoff made it almost impossible. Only a chosen few, carefully vetted, were permitted to invest in his Investment Securities, which Madoff ran like an exclusive country club.

In essence Madoff ran a classic Ponzi scheme, whereby high interest rates are paid to each generation of investors not out of profits, but out of the capital sums paid by subsequent generations. Ponzi's victims were his fellow Italian–Americans; Madoff's were his fellow Jews. There is little that is new in crime.

Madoff founded his Wall Street firm with capital of $5,000 in 1960, and remained its chairman until his arrest in December 2008. During that period, he built up a $700 million investment empire, with other assets (houses, yachts, jewellery, and works of art) worth at least $110 million. For a time, Madoff Securities was the sixth largest market maker on Wall Street, gaining Madoff the reputation of being a financial genius.

Some of his fortune was put to good use. Madoff was a philanthropist who donated money to medical, educational and cultural charities. Some of it was used to help Madoff gain access to Washington lawmakers and law regulators – he was a regular donor to both the Republican and Democratic Parties.

Unlike Ponzi, Madoff admitted his guilt, but not until after his sons had reported him to the federal authorities, and he had pocketed his annual bonus two months earlier than usual. The dominoes then fell swiftly. In February 2009, Madoff was banned for life from the securities industry. The following month he was remanded in custody, and in June, he was ordered to forfeit $170 billion in assets, and was sentenced to 150 years' imprisonment.

Bernie Madoff

Bernie Madoff is securely helped from a limousine on arrival at the Manhattan Federal Court, New York City on March 12, 2009. He was scheduled to plead guilty to a multi-billion dollar scheme to defraud investors.

Miscarriages of Justice?

Gerry Conlon squats by the grave of his father, Guiseppe.
Conlon spent 15 years in prison falsely accused, along with his
father, of a series of pub bombings in England in 1974. His
father died in prison.

Few grieved when the body of Russian immigrant and slum landlord, Leon Beron, was discovered on Clapham Common on New Year's Day 1911. He had been killed by a blow to the head, and a curious "S" mark had been carved on each of his cheeks – "like the f holes on a violin", remarked the police surgeon. Beron's wallet had been emptied.

One week later, the police arrested Steinie Morrison, another Russian immigrant and a professional thief. They made the arrest on a welter of circumstantial evidence – Morrison had been seen eating with Beron; Morrison had been working near Clapham Common; Morrison had lodged a revolver and 45 bullets in the left luggage office of St. Mary's Station, Whitechapel; a cabman claimed to have picked up Morrison from Clapham Common on the night of the murder, and that Morrison had plenty of money with him. It was pointed out at Morrison's trial that this witness came forward after Morrison's picture, and the offer of a reward, had appeared in newspapers. What counted more against Morrison was that he produced a false alibi, claiming he had been at the Shoreditch Empire at the time of Beron's murder.

Morrison was sent for trial. His barrister suggested that Beron had been a police informer, that the S marks stood for "spiccan" – the Polish word for a spy – and hinted at a conspiracy. This was, after all, the time of the Houndsditch murders and the hunt for the Russian anarchist gang led by Peter the Painter. It was to no avail. Morrison was found guilty. The judge pronounced the death sentence, "May the Lord have mercy on your soul" he added. "I decline such mercy," shouted Morrison. "I do not believe there is a God!" The Home Secretary, Winston Churchill, intervened. Churchill clearly had doubts about Morrison's guilt. Morrison's sentence was commuted to one of life imprisonment. Morrison, however, repeatedly asked to be put to death. On January 24, 1924, weakened by a series of hunger strikes, he died in Parkhurst Prison.

Steinie Morrison

An incorrectly labelled waxwork model of
Steinie Morrison in the Chamber of Horrors at
Madame Tussaud's, London.

THE ORIGINAL TREADM YORK REMOVED FROM

STINIE MORRISON

In 1912 Sir Arthur Conan Doyle, creator of the master detective Sherlock Holmes, published a book called *The Case of Oscar Slater*. It was not a work of fiction, but a book that demanded a re-examination of a murder that had taken place in a Glasgow apartment in Scotland three years earlier.

An elderly woman had been bludgeoned to death and robbed of a small diamond brooch. Witnesses disagreed as to the height and age of a man seen loitering near the apartment, but police decided that the culprit was Oscar Slater, a German Jew regarded by them as a "thoroughly bad lot". Slater had tried to sell a pawn ticket for a diamond brooch four days after the murder, and had then sailed with his girlfriend to the United States on the *SS Lusitania*. He was extradicted and brought to trial in the Edinburgh High Court on May 3, 1909.

His trial was a travesty of justice. It was proved that the pawn ticket related to a brooch pawned a month before the murder and that Slater had booked his ticket on the *Lusitania* six weeks before the murder. His alibi was dismissed. A majority of the jury found Slater guilty and he was sentenced to death. A petition for clemency raised 20,000 signatures. Two days before Slater was scheduled to die, the sentence was commuted to life imprisonment.

Conan Doyle then set to work. He discovered, among other things, that witnesses had been bribed to identify Slater and that Slater had a good alibi; that the victim almost certainly knew her murderer, and that she had not been killed with the hammer produced by the police but with a large chair. There were calls for a retrial, but it took another 15 years and another book for Slater to obtain justice. In 1927 a journalist named William Park published *The Truth About Oscar Slater*. A few weeks later Slater was released and pardoned. He received no compensation.

Oscar Slater

Oscar Slater leaves the forecourt of the Palace of Westminster shortly after his release from prison, August 2, 1928. He had served 19 years for a murder he did not commit.

Margaretha Geertruida Zelle was born in the Netherlands in 1876. As a young woman she went to live in Java, where she learnt something of Oriental dancing and entered into an unsuccessful marriage with a Dutch naval officer. With her liking for men of power and her developing talents as an exotic dancer, it was natural that she should make her way to Paris, and here she earned her living as courtesan, artists' model and dancer, changing her name to Mata Hari – Indonesian for "Eye of the Day". She was not classically beautiful, but she was attractive and decidedly arousing. She made friends, and also enemies – for she gained a reputation as a wanton and promiscuous woman.

As a citizen of the neutral Netherlands, Mata Hari travelled with relative freedom during World War I, moving between France and Germany via Spain and England. She told the British that she was a French agent, but the French authorities never supported this story. Then in January 1917, the German military attaché in Madrid transmitted messages to Berlin praising the activities of a spy with the code-name H-21. The messages were intercepted, and since they were transmitted in a code which the Germans knew had been broken, the French were able to read them and identify H-21 as Mata Hari.

On February 13, 1917, she was arrested in her Paris hotel room. She was put on trial, accused among other things of being responsible for the deaths of tens of thousands of French soldiers. She was found guilty and sentenced to death by firing squad.

Romantic legends clothe her execution. She is said to have blown a kiss to her executioners, to have flung open her coat and revealed her naked body, to have murmured as her last words "Merci, monsieur." There is even a story, reminiscent of Puccini's *Tosca*, that the firing squad had been bribed to use blanks. What is known is that she was shot on October 15, 1917.

Mata Hari

A discreetly dressed Mata Hari on the day of her arrest for spying, 1917.

On the night of the Reichstag fire in Berlin, February 27, 1933, the massive German chemical company I. G. Farben was holding a conference at the Hotel Adlon. Seeing the flames and the light in the sky, the industrialist Carl Duisberg turned to a colleague and said: "This fire will be a beacon to lead all Germany into the arms of Communism in years to come." Duisberg was mistaken. Although the Nazis had been responsible for the fire, their intention had been that the Communists were to be blamed. While the fire still blazed Göring ordered the arrest of all leading Communists, including members of the Reichstag.

Early in 1933 the Nazis stood on the threshold of power. Although he had been defeated by Hindenburg in the presidential election, Hitler had been appointed Chancellor of Germany on January 30. What was needed was the injection of terror into political life, the unmasking of some plot by the Nazis' strongest opposition – the Communists. A scapegoat for the arson of the Reichstag was found in Marinus van der Lubbe, a simple-minded Dutch Communist. Van der Lubbe was a strong young man, whose nickname was "Dempsey", after the American boxer, Jack Dempsey. After quarrelling with his sister, van der Lubbe drifted from his home town of Oegstgeest to Leiden, where he learned to speak German. He had a habit of assuming the blame for things that were not his fault – the organization of strikes, trouble at the workplace – and this, coupled with his known opposition to the Nazi Party, made him the ideal dupe for the Reichstag Fire.

He was arrested, given the semblance of a trial and sentenced to death. On January 10, 1934, three days before his 25th birthday, van der Lubbe was guillotined – the traditional means of execution in Germany at the time. He was then buried in an unmarked grave in Leipzig. By then, the Nazis had already been in power for an entire year.

Reichstag Fire

The Reichstag in flames on the night of February 27, 1933.
There would be a lot more burning in the years to come.

The crime was horrendous, but the case is remembered not for the crime, but for the punishment. Rainey Bethea was hanged in front of a crowd of 15,000 people in Owensboro, Kentucky, on August 14, 1936.

Bethea was a young black who had arrived in Owensboro three years earlier and had already had trouble with the law. In April 1935, he stole two purses from the Vogue Beauty Shop. As their value was over $25, he was convicted of grand larceny and sentenced to a year in the State Penitentiary. On his release, he returned to Owensboro, where he was convicted of being drunk and disorderly a month later. Since he couldn't pay the $100 fine – at the time he was making $7 a week – he was imprisoned for three months. Early on the morning of June 7, 1936, he was drunk again. He broke into the home of Lischia Edwards, entering via her bedroom window. The old lady woke. Bethea strangled her, raped her, and then searched through her jewellery – removing his own black celluloid prison ring as he did so. He took what he wanted, left his own ring, and fled, hiding the jewels in a barn not far away.

When Lischia Edwards' body was discovered, the Coroner was summoned. It was he who found Bethea's ring. A week later Bethea was arrested as he boarded a river barge. To their credit, the police did all they could to prevent him being lynched, for the woman he had killed was white, and local feeling ran high. Bethea made a full confession, but said that he did not know whether his victim was alive when he raped her. This was a significant point, for in Kentucky in 1936 it was not illegal to have intercourse with a corpse. The nature of his crime also posed a problem for the prosecution. The death penalty for murder and robbery was administered by the electric chair; for rape, by hanging. Bethea was tried for rape, and it took the jury less than five minutes to find him guilty.

Last American Public Hanging

The public hanging of Rainey Bethea, August 14, 1936. On the scaffold G. Phil Hanna is placing the noose around Bethea's neck.

The death penalty is a primitive means of exercising justice, and an even more primitive means of effecting a miscarriage of justice. When it is available to society, there are times when the urge to put someone to death seems to outrun logic and a proper appraisal of evidence by public, police and court alike. This is what happened in the first part of the English case that came to be known as 10 Rillington Place.

The London house was dark and dirty. In the late 1940s, it was occupied by John and Ethel Christie, on the ground floor, and by Timothy and Beryl Evans with their one-year-old daughter Geraldine on the top floor. The middle floor was unoccupied. In 1949 Beryl became pregnant. She was distraught. Having another baby would mean giving up her part-time job and the Evanses were already short of money. Abortion was then illegal, but Christie persuaded her that he could perform the operation in his flat. On November 8, Evans returned from work to be told by Christie that the operation had gone wrong and Beryl was dead. Christie also said that Geraldine was staying with a couple in Acton, and suggested that Evans leave London.

Evans did as he was told, but three weeks later gave himself up to the police in Wales. He was a man of limited intelligence who then made a series of mistakes. He changed his story repeatedly: now saying Beryl had died after taking something to procure a miscarriage, now implicating Christie, now saying that he had killed both his wife and daughter. The police found bodies hidden in the washhouse to the rear of the house, but failed to spot a human thigh bone resting against the fence.

Evans was poorly defended in court. The jury was not presented with important evidence. Evans was found guilty of the murder of Geraldine, and on March 9, 1950, was hanged at Pentonville

10 Rillington Place

The rubbish-strewn back garden of the sinister house at 10 Rillington Place where John Christie killed and buried his victims, April 1953.

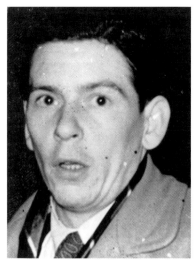

Prison. Two years passed, and then events moved swiftly. Ethel Christie disappeared, as did three London prostitutes. Christie's flat began to exude a most unpleasant smell, and he decided to leave. The new tenant of the top flat was given permission to clear out the ground floor kitchen. When he ripped the paper from the wall, he discovered a hidden pantry. In it was a body, dressed only in bra and stockings.

The police now found the bodies of Ethel, the three prostitutes, and two other women whom Christie had murdered in 1943–1944. Christie was arrested 10 days later. He was hanged on July 15, 1953, also at Pentonville. In 1966 Timothy Evans was granted a posthumous pardon. He would have been 46 years old.

(*left*) The hidden alcove where five bodies were found. (*above*) Timothy Evans, wrongly convicted of the murder of his own baby. (*below left*) John Reginald Halliday Christie, March 1953. (*opposite*) Christie arrives at the Old Bailey to face four charges of murder.

On November 2, 1952, Christopher Craig and Derek Bentley broke into a warehouse in Croydon, South London. Craig was armed with a gun and a knife. Bentley, who had a mental age of 12, probably did not know this. The police arrived and grabbed Bentley. Craig produced the gun, and Bentley called out: "Let him have it, Chris." Craig opened fire, wounding one policeman and killing another. Having exhausted his ammunition, Craig jumped from the roof, fracturing his spine and his left wrist. He was then arrested.

The crime itself was almost run-of-the-mill – murder during the course of a robbery. What made the case very special indeed was the trial and subsequent execution of Bentley. Craig was under age, and could not be sentenced to death even if convicted of murder. His sentence was "to be detained at Her Majesty's Pleasure". He was eventually released in 1962. Bentley, however, was over 18 and his life was at stake. Logic suggested that several defences might be open to Bentley. He was mentally retarded. He had not fired the fatal shot. It was never proved that he knew Craig was armed when they set out that night. None of these defences was accepted at his trial. It took the jury just 75 minutes to find both Craig and Bentley guilty of murder. Bentley was sentenced to death by Lord Chief Justice Goddard, a judge with an appetite for executions.

Bentley's appeal was turned down. The Home Secretary, another believer in executions, refused to seek clemency from the Queen. On January 28, 1953, Bentley was hanged in Wandsworth Prison. For 40 years his sister Iris fought for a posthumous pardon. It came in 1993. Five years later, the Court of Appeal overturned Bentley's conviction, Lord Chief Justice Bingham ruling that Bentley had been denied "that fair trial that is the right of every British citizen". To this day, no one knows what Bentley meant by "Let him have it, Chris." Was he urging Craig to fire? Or was he begging Craig to hand the gun to the police?

Bentley and Craig

Notice of the execution of Derek Bentley (*inset*) is posted outside Wandsworth Prison, January 28, 1953. Opponents of capital punishment are responsible for the broken glass.

James Hanratty was executed on April 4, 1962, following a clumsy investigation and a trial which was prosecuted with rare ferocity. Almost 50 years after the event, argument rages as to whether he was guilty, and there is certainly cause for doubt. There was another prime suspect who admitted the offence whereas Hanratty professed his innocence to the end. Hanratty also had an alibi confirmed by witnesses. Sadly he had more than one, which may well have convinced the jury that he was lying. Although a recent re-examination of the case has produced DNA evidence to suggest that he was guilty, it is quite likely that this evidence has been contaminated.

The facts of the killing are unchallenged. On August 22, 1961, Michael Gregsten and Valerie Storey were making love in Gregsten's car on the edge of a cornfield north of London, when a man with a gun got into the car. What followed was a nightmare – five hours of threats and madness, and an aimless drive into North London, back out to St. Albans, and finally to a lay-by on the A6 trunk road. Here the gunman raped Storey and, perhaps accidentally, shot and killed Gregsten. He then ordered Storey to drag her lover's body out of the car and, in total darkness, fired the rest of his bullets in her direction. She was hit in the legs and paralysed. The gunman drove off, crashing the gears. Five hours later, Storey was found by a farm labourer.

On October 11, James Hanratty, a professional car thief, was arrested in Blackpool and charged with Gregsten's murder. The case was originally set for the Old Bailey, but was unaccountably moved to Bedford. Evidence went missing, important papers were carelessly strewn across the courtroom floor and not subsequently examined. Understandably, given her ordeal and the darkness in which it took place, Storey gave conflicting descriptions of her attacker. No convincing motive was found for Hanratty to have committed the crime. Nevertheless, after nine hours' deliberation, the jury found him guilty. Despite an appeal and widespread protest, he was hanged at Bedford Jail, still declaring he was innocent.

A6 Murder

The famous lay-by off the A6, scene of the murder of
Michael Gregsten on August 22, 1961.

At first sight, the bodies of the three victims would have suggested that they had nothing in common save their youth – Chaney was 21, Schwerner was 24, Goodman was 20. One was a black Mississippian, one was a Jewish activist, one was from an upper-middle-class New York family. All three were found in an earthen dam on the Old Jolly Farm in Neshoba County, Mississippi, a state described by Martin Luther King Jnr. in his famous "I have a dream…" speech as "sweltering in injustice". They had been shot, and from the state of the bodies the shooting had taken place several weeks earlier. What the three young victims shared, however, was a passionate belief in the U.S. Civil Rights Movement of the 1960s.

On June 21, 1964, they had been preparing for the opening of a Freedom School in a church that had been firebombed by the Ku Klux Klan. Driving back to their office they were arrested by Deputy Sheriff Cecil Price, held for a while, then released when it was dark. A white mob was waiting for them. At 2.00 am Buford Posey, a local member of the NAACP (National Association for the Advancement of Colored People), was called by Edgar Ray Killen, the "chaplain" of the KKK and a part-time preacher. "We took care of your three friends tonight," said Killen, "and you're next." Posey called the FBI.

James Jordan, a Klan member, agreed to co-operate with the FBI. In the belief that no Mississippi jury would convict those responsible for the murders, the FBI decided that the charge would be conspiracy to deprive the three victims of their civil rights. Those charged included Deputy Sheriff Price and Sheriff Lawrence Rainey, both members of the KKK. On October 21, 1967, Jordan and Price were convicted and sentenced to four years and six years respectively. Rainey and Killen were acquitted, one of the jurors saying that there was no way she could convict a preacher.

Mississippi Burning

Members of the Mississippi Freedom Democratic Party hold banners of the slain volunteers, (left to right) Andrew Goodman, James Chaney and Michael Schwerner.

Another 38 years passed before Edgar Killen was brought to trial. On June 21, 2005 – the 41st anniversary of the killings – the jury returned their verdict on the three charges of murder and manslaughter against him. They found him guilty of the manslaughter of Chaney, Schwerner and Goodman. Killen was 80 years old at the time of his trial, confined to a wheelchair and breathing oxygen. He remained unrepentant, branding his victims from all those years ago as "Communists", who were threatening Mississippi's way of life.

(*clockwise from opposite top*) The burnt-out station wagon, in which Chaney, Goodman and Schwerner were last seen alive, dumped in the Bogue Chitto swamp. Investigators uncover remains of the three victims, August 28, 1963. Preacher and former Klansman Edgar Ray Killen at his trial for the murders of the three civil rights workers in June 2005.

For the first 50 years of it, Claus von Bulow's life was a series of smooth transitions. He went from privileged childhood to wealth and prestige via Trinity College, Cambridge, England, legal training, and employment as personal assistant to J. Paul Getty – and all this against the setting of Newport, Rhode Island. When he married Martha Crawford – known as Sunny – in 1966, two fortunes combined, for she had previously been the wife of Prince Alfred of Auersperg. There was nothing to suggest that life should ever be anything but extremely pleasant for the rich, handsome couple on their opulent estate at Clarendon Court.

Every silver lining has a cloud, however, and Sunny suffered from diabetes and depression. Some said she was at times suicidal. In 1980 her condition suddenly deteriorated to the point where she went into a coma. The police investigated this tragedy, became suspicious and arrested von Bulow. In 1982 he was brought to trial, accused of attempting to murder Sunny by administering an overdose of insulin, the alleged motive being that he wished to marry his long-term mistress, Alexandra Isles, a TV actress who had starred in the cult 1960s soap opera *Dark Shadows*. Von Bulow was found guilty and sentenced to 30 years in prison.

He immediately appealed, hiring as his attorney Alan Dershowitz, a Professor of Law at Harvard University. Dershowitz was able to cast considerable doubt on the reliability of much of the evidence at the first trial, and von Bulow's conviction was reversed in 1984. A second trial followed in 1985, and von Bulow was found "not guilty" on all charges.

Members of Sunny's family still had their doubts. For endorsing her father's innocence Cosima von Bulow – daughter of Claus and Sunny – was disinherited by her grandmother, Sunny's mother. At the same time, Sunny's two daughters by her previous marriage sued von Bulow for $56 million. The family feuds remain unresolved, and Sunny died in 2008.

Claus von Bulow

The millionaire and socialite Claus von Bulow at home in October 1985, following his second trial for the attempted murder of his wife.

It played like a soap opera. For months the most compelling viewing on television was the O.J. Simpson show. The images of bloodstained bodies, of the fugitive batting along the freeway with scores of police cars in hot pursuit, and the ensuing courtroom drama had all America, and much of the rest of the world, spellbound. Long before any evidence had been presented in court, millions of people knew what they wanted the verdict to be. On the one side were those who believed that the first pro-footballer to rush 2,000 yards in a single American League season could not possibly have murdered his wife. On the other side were those who believed that, O. J. was too popular, too rich, and just too "nice" for his own good, and that he was therefore guilty as charged. Logic had little to do with either decision. Race may well have had much to do with both decisions.

The simple fact was that Simpson's estranged second wife, Nicole Brown Simpson, and her friend Ronald Goldman were stabbed to death on June 12, 1994. Their bodies were found in the courtyard of Nicole Brown's condominium in Brentwood, California. The next day, Simpson left Chicago and returned to Los Angeles, where he was taken in by the LAPD for questioning. On June 17, the day of the funerals of the victims, Simpson made what appeared to be an attempt at flight in his white Ford Bronco, driven by a friend named A. C. Cowlings. He was pursued and taken into custody. On July 22, Simpson pleaded "absolutely 100 per cent not guilty" to two counts of first-degree murder.

The criminal trial opened five months later, on January 24, 1995, before Judge Lance A. Ito and a jury of eight blacks, one white, one Hispanic, and two jurors of mixed race. Marcia Clark led for the prosecution, Johnnie Cochran for the defense. It was a sensation. A cast selected from the cream of Hollywood could not have played it better, and viewing figures for what amounted

O. J. Simpson

The LAPD mugshot of O. J. Simpson.

to a new TV soap opera hit the roof. Simpson must have taken some comfort from the knowledge that the prosecution was not seeking the death penalty. His book *I Want To Tell You* was published at the height of the trial.

The soap's most dramatic moment came on May 15 when Simpson was asked to put on the bloodstained Aris Light gloves that had been found at the scene of the murders, and were assumed to be those of the murderer. They did not fit. They were too small. "I don't think he could act the size of his hands," said Cochran. "He would be a great actor if he could act his hands larger."

More than half the population of the United States saw the jury foreman deliver the verdict live on television – "not guilty". Simpson's life since then has slid downhill. In 1997 a civil jury found him liable for the wrongful death of Ronald Goodman, and ordered him to pay over $33 million in damages. Friends melted away. Simpson turned to crime. He was convicted of armed robbery and conspiracy to kidnap, and in December 2008 he was sentenced to at least seven years in prison. He is currently serving his sentence at the Lovelock Correctional Center, Nevada.

(*clockwise from bottom right*) The bloodstained front path to the home of Nicole Brown Simpson, June 14, 1994. A photo of Nicole Brown taken after her 911 call reporting domestic violence back in January 1989, and shown in court during O. J. Simpson's trial. The Ford Bronco and escort on Highway 405, June 17, 1994. Prosecutor Christopher Darden (far right) looks impassively on as Simpson shows the extra large Aris gloves that didn't fit, June 21, 1995.

(*opposite*) Supporters and fans of O. J. Simpson cele-
brate after watching the end of the trial on television,
October 2, 1995. (*above*) The team wins through…
Simpson and his leading attorneys F. Lee Bailey (left)
and Johnnie Cochran (right) hear the jury's "not guilty"
verdict.

Mobsters and Monsters

Over 100 members of the Sicilian Mafia in cages in
court in Catanzaro, Italy, on November 1, 1967.
They were on trial for assorted crimes.

In a century that many perceived as the most violent in history, one man of violence achieved a unique fame. Sixty years after his death, Alphonse Capone remains the most notorious gangster and mobster of all time. He was a man with great physical strength – capable of clubbing people to death with a single blow – considerable intelligence, and no scruples whatsoever. At the height of his power he controlled gambling houses, race tracks, brothels, speakeasies, nightclubs, distilleries and breweries, with interests in a number of legitimate enterprises.

He was born in Brooklyn on January 17, 1899. In this tough neighbourhood he joined a couple of "kid gangs" known as the Brooklyn Rippers and the Forty Thieves Juniors, before graduating to work as a bouncer and bartender at Frankie Yale's Harvard Inn. For all its fancy title, it was a rough joint, and it was here that Capone was cut about the face by an angry customer, thus gaining his lifelong nickname "Scarface". Capone always gave as good as he got, however, and in 1919 Yale sent Capone and his family to Chicago, the idea being that they would stay there until things cooled down.

Capone and the Chicago of the Roaring Twenties were made for each other. On Yale's advice, he joined John Torrio's gang, soon taking over as leader when Torrio was wounded in an assassination attempt by a rival gang and decided to retire. By the late Twenties, Capone's income was reckoned to be $100 million a year – on which he paid no income tax. Life was good. There was only one drawback. Although the Mayor of Chicago, "Big Bill" Hale Johnson Jnr. was corrupt, he drew the line at working with Capone, claiming that the mobster was bad for his political image. Capone had to look elsewhere for a family home, and eventually bought a property in Palm Island, Florida.

Al Capone

Alphonse "Scarface" Capone hits the big time and makes the cover of *Time* magazine, March 24, 1930.

TIME

The Weekly Newsmagazine

ALPHONSE ("SCARFACE") CAPONE
A pink apron, a pan of spaghetti.
(See NATIONAL AFFAIRS)

It was a convenient location for an alibi. On a freezing cold St. Valentine's Day in 1929, the rivalry between Capone and Bugs Moran came to a head. Capone's henchman Jack McGurn led a team of four hit-men to wipe out Moran at the SMC Company Garage at 2122 North Clark. The bait was a fake bootlegging deal that Moran was unlikely to refuse – a delivery of whiskey. McGurn's men arrived in a stolen police car, and Moran, believing a real raid was in progress, slipped away. Six members of his gang, and one innocent bystander, entered the garage and were slaughtered. The finger pointed at Capone. It was a classic Capone-style hit. But Capone had been a thousand miles away, sunning himself in Florida.

Capone was seldom in jail. He was arrested in 1926 for killing three people, but spent only one night behind bars. Three months after the St. Valentine's Day Massacre, he was imprisoned for carrying a gun. Despite being top of the list of Chicago's Most Wanted Criminals in 1930, Capone remained free to walk the blood-splattered streets, but the success of Capone's business enterprises was about to catch up with him. In 1931, he was indicted for income tax evasion. The government charged that he owed $215,000 in back taxes from his gambling profits. Capone pleaded guilty in the belief that he would be able to plea bargain.

Judge James H. Wilkerson refused to cut a deal. Capone changed his plea to "not guilty" and tried to bribe the jury, but Wilkerson switched the jury at the last minute. Capone was found guilty on just five of the 23 counts against him. It was enough. He was sentenced to a total of 10 years in federal prison and one year in the county jail.

In jail, Capone was a model prisoner. He furnished his cell with rugs, a typewriter and a complete set of the

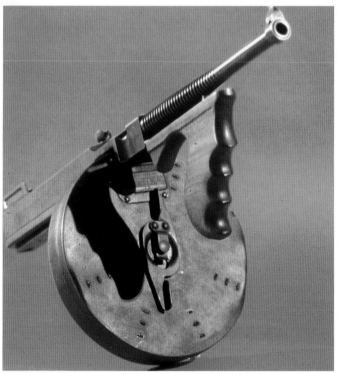

(*clockwise from top left*) Bugs Moran, leader of the North Side Gang in Chicago, 1928. Members of Moran's mob, and one innocent bystander, lie on the floor of the garage at 2122 North Clark, February 14, 1929. The gun said to have been used by Capone on one of the rare occasions when he pulled the trigger. "Machine Gun Jack" McGurn with his wife "the blonde alibi" Louise Rolf on February 15, 1936 – McGurn worked for Capone and led the team of hit-men that wiped out Moran.

Encyclopedia Britannica, and refused to take part in any strikes or prison riots. He served most of his sentence in Alcatraz, much of it in the hospital, for he was diagnosed as suffering from syphilitic dementia.

He was released in November 1939 and returned to his home in Palm Island. The dementia worsened and Capone was forced to live a quiet life. On January 21, 1947, he suffered an apoplectic stroke unrelated to his syphilis,

contracted pneumonia and died four days later of cardiac arrest. He was initially buried at the centre of his empire, on Chicago's South Side, but a year later his remains were removed to Mount Carmel Cemetery on the West Side.

To many, he is still the greatest mobster of all time.

QUI RIPOSA
GABRIELE CAPONE
NATO DIC....
O NOV 14, 1920
QUI RIPOSA
SALVATORE CAPONE
NATO TURINO 16, 1895
MORTE APRILE 1, 192

AL CAPONE
1899 — 1947

REST IN PEACE
CAPONE

(*left to right from far left*) The law enforcer and leader of The Untouchables, Eliot Ness, sits at his desk in the early 1930s. Capone plays cards in a train transporting him to prison, October 1931. Al Capone's tombstone in Mount Carmel Cemetery, June 1948.

By the time he was 14, Arthur Flegenheimer had worked out that he would never get rich through honest toil. Three months later he received his first and only prison sentence, which he served on Blackwell's Island, a brutal institution on New York's East River. On his release, his fellow Bronx gang members gave him his professional name – "Dutch Schultz".

Dutch was a mobster in the roughest mould. He had no sense of compromise, no belief in negotiation. He was a "fight or flight" guy, never seeking some other solution to any problem he faced. He made vast fortunes in bootlegging, an estimated $12 million to $15 million a year from the numbers racket, and plenty more from protection rackets and manipulation of labour unions. He shunned smart clothes. Lucky Luciano called him "one of the cheapest guys I ever knew... a guy with a couple of million bucks and he dressed like a pig".

Dutch was also a vicious man. In his early bootleg days, Dutch kidnapped a rival beer-baron named Joe Rock, hung him by his thumbs on a meat hook, and allegedly then blindfolded Rock's eyes with gauze that had been smeared with the discharge from a gonorrhoea infection. Rock lost his sight. When Dutch learned that a partner had been creaming money from the take, he whipped out a gun in the presence of his astonished lawyer, stuck it in the partner's mouth and pulled the trigger. Later, he took time to cut out the victim's heart.

He trusted no one, had no friends. In the end, it was a race between the law and other mobsters as to who would get him first. The mobsters won. On October 23, 1935, Charles Workman, a gunman hired by Murder Inc., walked into the Palace Chop House looking for Dutch. He found him in the men's room. The one bullet that hit Dutch ripped through his abdomen, large intestine, gall bladder, and liver. Dutch died 12 hours later. In what was seen as a deliberate snub to this unlovable man, his fellow mobsters sent only four floral tributes to his funeral.

Dutch Schultz

Arthur Simon Flegenheimer, professionally known as Dutch Schultz, awaits the verdict in a tax case against him. This time he got away with it.

Francesco Castiglia was four years old when his family emigrated from Calabria to the States in 1895. His early criminal training took place in New York's East Harlem, where he changed his name to Frank Costello and with the coming of Prohibition in 1919, he was ready to join forces with Lucky Luciano in bootlegging and gambling enterprises. As the years passed, Costello gained a reputation as being the guy who could buy-off anyone – police, politicians, even judges. In 1936, when Luciano was sent to Dannemora prison in upstate New York, he chose Costello as the family's acting boss. Costello didn't let him down, increasing profits across the country – from slot machines in New Orleans, gambling in Florida (with Meyer Lansky), and illegal race wires in LA (with Bugsy Siegel).

An intense rivalry developed between Costello and Luciano's other lieutenant, Vito Genovese. For a while this didn't matter, for Genovese fled from the States in 1951 fearing that he was about to be charged with murder. Six years later, however, he was back. Genovese hired Vincente "The Chin" Gigante to get rid of Costello, but Gigante made the mistake of shouting "Frank, this is for you!" just before he pulled the trigger. Costello spun round, ducked, and the shots merely grazed his head. Gigante fled, and later turned himself in to the police.

Costello and Genovese came to terms. Genovese wished to deal with the other family member that he loathed, Albert Anastasia. When Anastasia was gunned down on October 25, 1957, Costello called up his old associates Luciano and Lansky. Together they framed Genovese, Gigante and Carmine Galante so that all three went down on a drugs charge. Genovese died in prison. Costello remained busy, operating from New York's Waldorf Astoria until he died of a heart attack in 1973. When Carmine Galante was released from prison, he paid his respects to the man who had framed him by blowing up the doors to Costello's tomb.

Frank Costello

Frank Costello draws comfort during a Senate hearing on organized gambling, 1950.

alvatore Luciana was born in Sicily, Italy, in 1896 and arrived in New York 10 years later. It did not take long for him to team up with two other kids, named Meyer Lansky and Bugsy Siegel, and start a two-cent protection racket. The trio prospered and, within a year of the introduction of Prohibition, Charles Luciano (as he was now known) was working as a bootlegger for Frank Costello and Vito Genovese.

After a spell in jail, Luciano joined Joe Masseria's gang, becoming second-in-command in 1925. Four years later open warfare broke out between Masseria and a rival Sicilian gang led by Salvatore Maranzano. Luciano was captured by Maranzano's men who stabbed him with an ice pick, slit his throat, and left him for dead on Staten Island beach. It was his miraculous survival that earned him the name "Lucky" Luciano.

Lucky was ambitious. In April 1931 Joe Masseria was killed in a Coney Island restaurant while Luciano, in true Pontius Pilate style, washed his hands in the bathroom. He now became Maranzano's second-in-command, but not for long. Luciano and Lansky learned that Maranzano was planning to have three men eliminated – Al Capone, Vito Genovese, and Lucky himself. Four of Lansky's associates raided Maranzano's office and killed him. On their way in they met Vincent "Mad Dog" Coll, the man Maranzano had hired to kill Luciano. Not knowing who he was they simply told Coll that they were government agents. Coll fled.

Luciano had what he wanted. He was top man in New York, but had a greater sense of diplomacy than most Mafia leaders. He divided the city into several territories, each controlled by a different Family, under the control of La Commissione, a governing body presided over by Luciano. The system was effective, but in 1936 Luciano was found guilty, on perjured evidence, of

Lucky Luciano

Lazy-eyed and full of menace – a portrait of Lucky Luciano from 1935.

procuring for immoral purposes and was sentenced to between 30 and 50 years in jail.

Luciano spent World War II in prison, arranging Mafia assistance for the U.S. government and U.S. forces in Italy, clearing the way for the invasion of Sicily, and easing the progress of U.S. troops as they fought their way through Italy. At the same time, he used his Mafia connections to remove Communist influence in the Italian resistance and local government.

In return, the patriot mobster was paroled immediately after the war, on condition that he returned to Italy. Luciano agreed, stopping off in Cuba for the famous Havana Conference where he and Lansky arranged the execution of their childhood playmate, Bugsy Siegel. There were numerous threats on Lucky's life subsequently, but when he died it was from a heart attack at Naples International Airport. His body was returned to the United States and buried in St. John's Cemetery, Queens.

(*top*) Luciano (third from right) enjoys a stroll through Lercara, Sicily, in 1949. (*below*) In busier days, Luciano (hands to face) is booked at a New York City courtroom desk early in 1935. (*opposite*) The luck runs out – the body of Charles "Lucy" Luciano lies on the ground at Naples Airport, January 26, 1962.

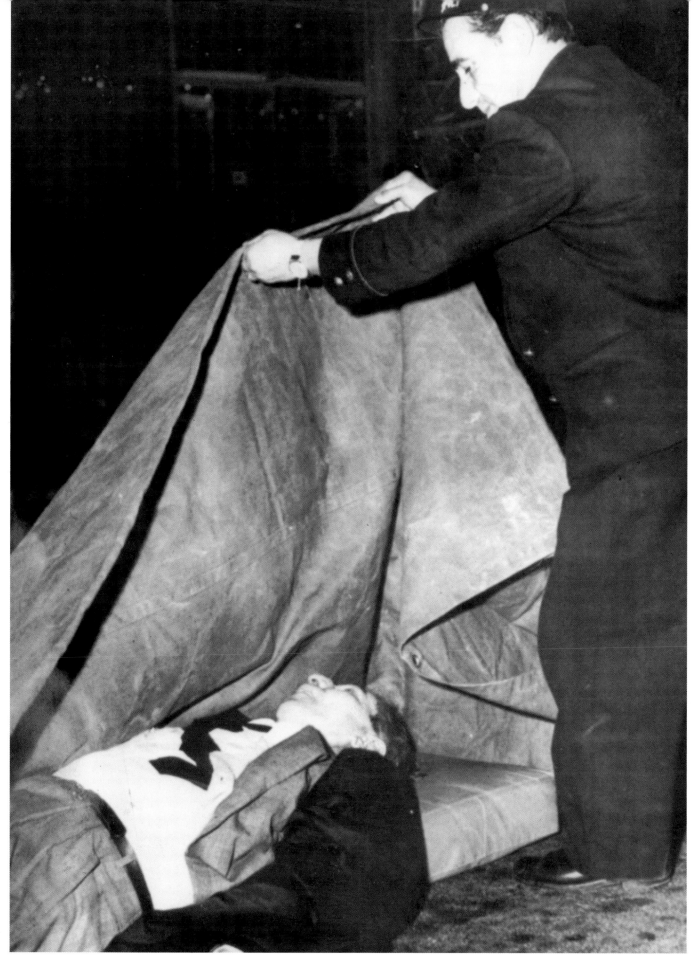

Benjamin Siegelbaum disliked his nickname intensely. It was wiser to call him "Ben", better still to call him "Mr Siegel". The first half of his short life was the routine mobster progression from rags to racketeering. He was born in 1905 in Hell's Kitchen, Brooklyn, where he ran protection rackets with a weak-willed friend named Moey Sedway, before meeting the man who was to be a major influence in his life and the instigator of his death – Meyer Lansky. Bugsy's first murder was a revenge killing. Lucky Luciano, an associate of Lansky, was sent down on a drugs charge. Bugsy and Lansky decided to execute the 19-year-old witness responsible for the conviction. The boy's body was never found. A local woman who claimed she had information on the killing was savagely beaten. Bugsy met the woman by chance eight years later, raped her and threatened her with worse if she went to the police.

Bugsy would have been just another vicious racketeer making money from bootlegging and gambling dens. What gave him a place in history began with his move to California in 1937. He bought a 35-room mansion in Hollywood, took control of the unions that supplied labour to the film industry, and slid into glamorous society. His good looks, considerable charm and ruthless business methods brought him the power to shut down every studio in town. At the same time he collected money from the stars to prevent him doing just that.

After World War II Bugsy hit on the idea of building a top hotel and casino in the sandy wastes of the Nevada Desert at a little place called Las Vegas. At first the project proved a nightmare, but by May 1947 both hotel and casino were up and running and Bugsy had cleared his debts. He had less than a month to enjoy his success. His old partner Meyer Lansky suspected that Bugsy was hiding some of the profits they were jointly making. On June 20, while he was relaxing in his Beverly Hills home, Bugsy was shot four times in the chest. He died almost instantly.

Bugsy Siegel

The man who made Las Vegas the gambling Mecca of the United States – Bugsy Siegel lights up at the height of his power, 1940.

The story of Ronnie and Reggie Kray, twins born just 10 minutes apart, has its contradictions. They were icons of the East End of London, the guardians of gangland law and order, and yet as children vastly preferred the country to the city. Their father and mother, whom the twins idolized, made them take up boxing to "keep them out of trouble", but it was in the ring that Ronnie, Reggie, and brother Charlie learned that an opponent is never beaten until he is totally broken. Both Ronnie and Reggie longed to have "class", fame, and a glittering lifestyle, though their natural milieu was the rough and ready world of gambling dens and shady clubs.

By the mid-1960s, the Krays had come a long way. They owned a smart club in Knightsbridge and were to be seen with celebrities from the worlds of sport and showbiz. In 1964, a newspaper hinted that Ronnie was having a homosexual affair with Lord Boothby, a former cabinet minister. Boothby was paid £40,000 in an out-of-court settlement, but knowledge that his homosexuality was now an open secret marked the beginning of Ronnie's progressive paranoia and an increasing violence in both the twins.

In the East End they were kings, but the Richardsons ruled south of the river, and the Thames did not keep the rival gangs apart. There were worsening disputes over the rackets that both gangs ran. During a gun battle in a club in Catford, the Krays' cousin Richard Hart was killed. This had to be avenged, and the gunman in the frame for Hart's death was George Cornell. In March 1966 Ronnie and Reggie learned that Cornell was drinking on their territory in a pub called The Blind Beggar. Ronnie set off. As he entered, Cornell greeted him sarcastically. Ronnie whipped out a pistol and fired three shots into Cornell's head. The East End kept its mouth shut.

The Krays

Ronnie (*right*) and Reggie Kray take a walk through their "manor" in 1965.

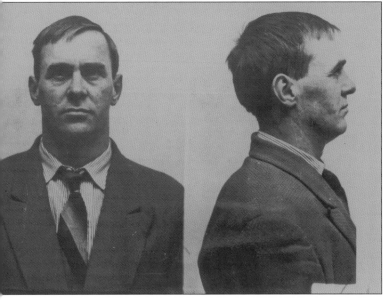

No action was taken by the police, but six months later came another killing. Jack "The Hat" McVitie had been paid by Ronnie to kill an informer named Leslie Payne. McVitie failed to kill Payne but kept the money. In October 1967 he was invited to a party. The twins arrived early, and persuaded the other guests to leave. When McVitie walked in, Reggie held a gun to his head and pulled the trigger. The gun jammed. It might have been better for McVitie if it hadn't. Reggie threw down the gun, drew a knife, and stabbed McVitie repeatedly in the face, chest and stomach.

The law was delighted to step in at last. Scotland Yard detectives had been longing to get their hands on the Krays for years. For the killings and a whole backlog of offences, Charlie received eight years, the twins a minimum of 30 years each. Their fans and supporters campaigned for

lesser sentences, arguing that the victims of the Krays were almost invariably fellow criminals, but the sentences remained. Ronnie died in prison in 1996. Reggie was released on compassionate grounds in 2000, to die of cancer six weeks later.

The East End gave him a great send-off.

(*above*) The 17-year-old Kray twins, with Reggie on the left, pose with their proud and devoted mother, Violet Kray in 1950. (*opposite, top*) Tough company… Ronnie (second from left) and Reggie pose with former gangster and film star George Raft (third from left) and World Heavyweight Champion Rocky Marciano (second from right). (*opposite, below*) George Cornell, murdered by Ronnie Kray in The Blind Beggar pub.

In 1951 a prison report on 17-year-old Charles Manson described him as "…a slick institution-alized youth… dangerous… should not be trusted across the street…" Seven years and several crimes later, Manson was said to be "… a very shaky probationer and it seems just a matter of time before he gets into further trouble". Up to this point, however, Manson's crimes had been of a comparatively petty nature – minor theft, driving a stolen car across state lines, assault and passing stolen cheques. Although he had spent almost half his life in prison, Manson was still a long way from deserving the title he was later given of "the symbol of ultimate evil".

Big trouble came in the 1960s. While serving a 10-year sentence on McNeil Island, Washington state, Manson raped another inmate at razor point. This was violence at a new level. Against his own wishes, Manson was released in March 1967, and moved to the Haight-Ashbury area of San Francisco where he began recruiting what others referred to as his "Family". With a group of some 30 hard-core followers, Manson left the city to take over a disused ranch in the San Fernando Valley. Here he cultivated a pseudo-religious status. He became interested in some of the weirder movements of the age – the Church of the Final Judgement, the Church of Satan, and the Circe Order of Dog Blood. He also encouraged his Family to believe that he was the reincarnation of Christ.

Then in August 1969, came the two nights when the Family indulged in an horrendous orgy of killing. At midnight on August 8, under orders from Manson, but without their leader's presence, a car load of his followers drove out to film director Roman Polanski's Beverly Hills home. Polanski was away, filming in London. It made no difference. The Family shot a friend of the gardener, then entered the house and rounded up the four occupants – Jay Sebring, Wojciech Frykowski, Abigail Folger and Sharon Tate. Sebring was shot, Frykowski was bludgeoned to

Charles Manson

The eyes and "x" scar on the forehead of Charles Manson, the cult-leader who claimed that he was "the mad dog killer fiend leper" that reflected the society he lived in.

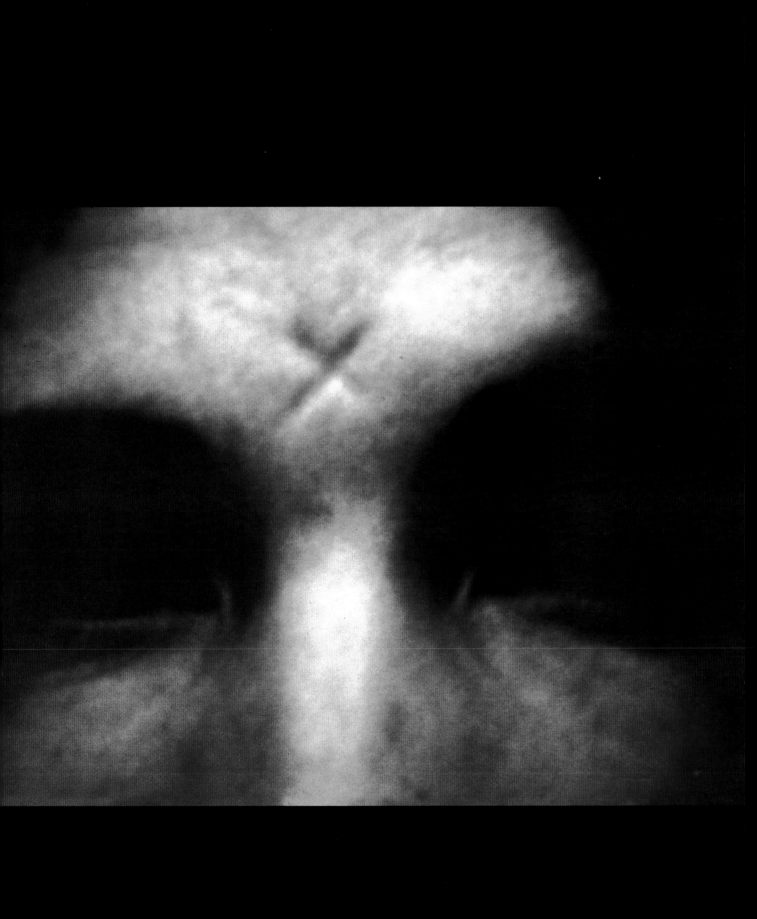

death, Folger was repeatedly stabbed. Sharon Tate, who was eight months pregnant, begged for the life of her unborn child. One of the killers, Susan Atkins, replied: "Look, bitch, I don't care if you are having a baby. You are going to die and I don't feel a thing about it." Atkins then stabbed her to death.

The following night, Manson took three members of the Family, two of whom had been involved in the previous killings, to the home of Leno and Rosemary LaBianca. Manson reportedly told his followers he was going "to show them how to do it", how to kill without indulging in such mayhem. No other motive for this crime has been discov-

ered. At Manson's trial it was suggested that he believed a global race war was imminent, which "the Blacks" would win. The Family would be able to sit out this war in peace in a secret underground world reached via a hole in the Californian desert, to emerge as leaders when the war was over. The Tate and La Bianca killings had taken place because "the Blacks" were unable or unwilling to precipitate the war, and had therefore to be shown how to do it.

On 29 March, 1971, Manson was sentenced to death. This was later commuted to life in prison after California's Supreme Court invalidated all death sentences imposed in the state prior to 1972. Manson remains in prison today. All

(*above*) The front yard of the Barker Ranch, Death Valley, California, where Manson and his Family lived through much of 1968 and 1969. It was owned by the grandmother of Catherine Gillies, a Family member. Manson sent Gillies to murder her grandmother, so that she could inherit the ranch, but the plot was foiled by a flat tyre. (*right*) The nearby Spahn's Movie Ranch, where the family lived before moving to Barker Ranch.

(*clockwise from top left*) The pregnant film star Sharon Tate, wife of the director Roman Polanski, holds up baby clothes in the back of a London taxi on August 6, 1969, three days before she was murdered. Susan Atkins, one of the killers of Sharon Tate. Roman Polanski sits on the bloodstained porch of his Californian home a few days after the murder of his wife, Sharon Tate. Two members of the Family in the early 1970s.

his applications for parole have been denied, the latest on March 24, 2007, the most famous that of 1986 when he appeared before the board with a swastika embossed on his forehead. It is unlikely that he will ever be released. It is said that he gets over 60,000 items of mail a year, much of it from young people who wish to join the Family.

The Family itself survives, and has committed other murders since Manson's incarceration. In September 1975, Lynette Alice "Squeaky" Fromme attempted to assassinate President Gerald Ford in Sacramento, but she had failed to ensure that her gun was loaded. She claimed that the reason for her attempt was that Manson would be called to appear as a witness at her trial and would thereby have a platform from which to reaffirm his apocalyptic vision.

The hole in the desert and the underground world to which it led have not yet been found.

In the late 1950s Jommie Jones established the People's Temple in Indianapolis, later moving to San Francisco. The Temple did not prosper. There were scandals, and by the early 1970s the movement was on the point of collapse. Jones decided to leave the United States and establish a utopian community in Guyana. It was named Jonestown. There were problems from the beginning – lack of adequate food, a brutal work regime, fevers and outbreaks of severe diarrhoea. Discipline was rigorously enforced by armed guards. Offenders were incarcerated in boxes or had electric shocks administered to their genitalia. Would-be deserters were incapacitated by drugs. It was said by survivors that there were beatings. Parents had to surrender guardianship of their children to Jones, who was addressed as "Dad" or "Father" by everyone.

In November 1978 the community was visited by Congressman Leo Ryan and a team of "Concerned Relatives of People's Temple Members", aiming to investigate alleged violations of human rights. Jones did all he could to disrupt the visit, and to give the false impression that all was well in Jonestown. He failed. Many members of the community begged Ryan to take them with him when it was time to leave. Fanatical followers of Jones attacked the plane as it prepared for take-off, killing Ryan, three journalists, a cameraman and three defectors.

Knowing what would follow, Jones decided to bring the dream-turned-nightmare to an end with a mass suicide. On November 18 a mixture of grape Flavor Aid laced with Valium and cyanide was dispensed to his followers in paper cups. Babies and children were the first to die. The deadly cocktail was squirted down their throats with syringes. Then came the elderly, and finally the adults. Many parents took the poison immediately after watching their children die. A few tried to flee. Most were shot by Jones's guards although a few managed to escape. Jones died from a gunshot in the head. It is not known if it was self-administered. All in all, 913 of the 1110 members died, including 276 children. Jonestown itself was destroyed by fire in the mid-1980s.

Jonestown

Bodies of men, women and children cover the ground at Jonestown following the largest mass suicide in modern history, November 18, 1978.

The Branch Davidian Seventh-Day Adventists were formed in 1959. By 1990 they were led by David Koresh, and their headquarters was a compound at Waco, Texas. At 9.30 am on February 28, 1993, agents of the Bureau of Alcohol, Tobacco and Firearms attempted to serve arrest and search warrants on Koresh and the compound. There was a gun battle. Four ATF agents were killed and 16 wounded. The number of Davidian casualties is not known. The Waco siege began.

It lasted 51 days. The ATF agents were joined by the FBI, Texas Rangers and police, with the FBI leading the operation. From time to time, children and other Davidians were released by Koresh, or managed to break out, but the authorities became impatient and uneasy. The Davidians were believed to have sufficient food and supplies to last them a year or more. There was talk of cutting off supplies of water and electricity to the compound, but pressure increased to use more direct action to end the stand-off. The besiegers brought up flammable tear-gas canisters and Bradley armoured vehicles.

On Sunday, April 18, the FBI warned the Davidians that a move would be made against the compound and ordered them to vacate the compound's tower. The Davidians refused, presenting children at the windows and holding up a sign saying "Flames Await". Early the following morning the assault began with a tear-gas attack that lasted three hours. The end came when flames appeared in the compound, although there is still bitter controversy as to which side started the fire. The White House insisted that those inside the compound were responsible. Others claimed that news footage of burning canisters being fired into the compound by the besiegers mysteriously disappeared after only one showing on TV. A total of 86 people were killed, including 17 children and Koresh himself. There were only nine survivors.

Waco and Aftermath

Flames engulf the observation tower at the Waco Compound, April 19, 1993. There is still controversy as to who started the fire – the besiegers or the besieged.

One of the visitors to Waco while the siege was in progress was a young ex-soldier and hero of the first Gulf War named Timothy McVeigh. Already hostile towards government agencies, McVeigh's anger at what he saw was to have terrifying consequences. On the second anniversary of the ending of the siege and the killing of the Davidians, McVeigh drove a truck up to the Alfred P. Murrah Federal Building in Oklahoma City, just as staff were arriving for work. The truck was loaded with a 5000 lb mixture of agricultural fertilizer and a highly volatile motor-racing fuel. McVeigh got out of the truck and a few moments later ignited a time fuse. Hundreds were injured and 168 men, women and children were killed.

In June 1997 he was convicted of the killing of eight federal employees, and was ultimately executed by lethal injection four years later. He was 33 years old.

(above) The north side of the Alfred P. Murrah Federal Building, Oklahoma City, April 19, 1995. At the time, it was the worst terror attack in history on American soil. (opposite) Timothy McVeigh, in orange prison uniform, arrives at the Oklahoma courthouse two years later. Following his conviction and death sentence, McVeigh initially appealed. In March 1999 the Supreme Court turned down his last appeal, though it was not until June 2001 that McVeigh was executed by lethal injection.

Until the late 1990s few people outside the Balkans had heard of Kosovo, a province of Serbia inhabited largely by ethnic Albanians. Throughout history, the Balkans had been a place of unrest, a vast mountainous cockpit in which war after war was fought, and the scene of numerous insurrections and nationalist rebellions. In the turmoil that followed the death of President Josip Tito of Yugoslavia in 1980, the constituent units of the Yugoslav Federation began to break from one another. In April 1991 open warfare broke out between the Bosnian government and local Serbs.

At the time, Slobodan Milosevic was President of the Serbian Republic. He was a man who held the Serbian cause high and who carried deeply-held grudges concerning the way history, and his country's neighbours, had treated Serbia. As with all wars, the longer fighting continued the more vicious it became, culminating in a series of atrocities, the most infamous of which was the mass slaughter of Albanians in the southern part of Kosovo in 1999. Dozens of men, women and children were killed. They were probably civilians, although the Serb police insisted that the men and boys were dressed in the uniform of the Kosovo Liberation Army. After death, the bodies had been mutilated. Eyes had been gouged. Heads had been smashed. Some of the victims had been decapitated.

The world was appalled. Milosevic was called upon to identify those responsible and ensure that they were brought to justice. When he failed to do this, he was himself indicted as a war criminal by the United Nations. In June 2001 he was handed over to the Hague Tribunal, but his spirited attacks on the validity of that court and his skilful use of delaying tactics, resulted in his trial not opening until February 2002. The United Nations Chief Prosecutor Carla del Ponte accused Milosevic of being responsible for "the worst crimes to humankind".

Slobodan Milosevic

Former Yugoslav President Slobodan Milosevic is portrayed as a saint on the walls of the Socialist Party Headquarters, Belgrade, March 13, 2006 – two days after his death.

With all this tension, Milosevic's health rapidly began to decline. He was ill for weeks at a time, suffering from heart trouble, high blood pressure and fatigue. Proceedings were further delayed when the trial's presiding judge resigned for undisclosed health reasons. By that time the trial had already produced over 630,000 pages of evidence and statements. It dragged on for a further four years.

In the end, death intervened. On March 11, 2006, a prison guard found Milosevic dead in his cell. Although his defence attorney suggested that he had been poisoned, it seems probable that ultimately his heart failed. He died leaving the future of Kosovo still the subject of intense dispute.

(*above*) Milosevic is led into the courtroom for his first appearance before the UN Crimes Tribunal at The Hague, July 3, 2001. (*opposite*) The "Death Notice" of Milosevic, placed by his daughter in the Montenegrin daily newspaper *Pobjeda*.

ТАТА

Волим те.

Твоја МАРИЈА

7460(п.в.)

The Columbine High School Massacre of 1999 was not a unique event. Throughout the 1990s there had been at least 20 incidents of armed attacks on schools by students, the great majority of them in the United States. What made Columbine different was that the killers were neither deranged strangers nor terrorists. For two years Eric Harris, one of the two killers, had been posting death threats against students and teachers at Columbine on his website. He and Dylan Klebold had been rehearsing the massacre. They had kept a journal outlining plans for a major bomb attack, to be followed by the hijacking of a plane at Denver International Airport. This was not to be used to escape, but was to be flown into a major building in New York City.

Harris and Klebold arrived at Columbine at 11.15 am on Tuesday April 20, 1999. They placed two bombs in the school cafeteria, and as they left Harris told Brooks Brown, a student against whom he had posted death threats on his website, to "get out of here". In the car park, Harris and Klebold armed themselves with two sawn-off shotguns, a semi-automatic rifle and a semi-automatic pistol. They climbed to the highest point on the campus, and began shooting at 11.19 am, killing three students and seriously injuring nine others. Klebold then descended the stairs leading to the cafeteria, shooting indiscriminately as he went, before he and Harris headed off towards the Library.

Inside the Library were 55 students, three library staff and one teacher. Harris ordered them all to stand up. Klebold shot one of the students. He and Harris sat down and reloaded their weapons. The cycle of taunting, shooting, killing and reloading continued for some 13 minutes, until Harris and Klebold had had enough.

Columbine and Beslan

A still from one of the five home-made videos shows Eric Harris (*left*) and Dylan Klebold at target practice six weeks before the Columbine High School massacre.

EXCLUSIVE

THE COLUMBINE TAPES

The killers tell why they did it

■ The five home videos they made before their death
■ What the families are doing to prevent another tragedy

The school-cafeteria surveillance video

(*clockwise from top left*) A still from the school cafeteria CCTV as Klebold and Harris begin their attack on fellow students, April 20, 1999. Traumatized students watch as the last of the survivors are evacuated from the school building. A 1998 Columbine High School Yearbook photo of Dylan Klebold. Eric Harris's photo from the 1999 Yearbook.

There were to be only two more deaths, those of Harris and Klebold themselves. For 20 minutes they wandered through the school, hurling bombs and shooting aimlessly into classrooms before returning to the Library. Here, 50 minutes after their arrival at school, they committed suicide, in each case with a single shot to the head. Another three hours were to pass before all the wounded survivors were able to get out of the building.

The appalling events at Beslan's Middle School Number One in Russia in the first week of September 2004 were on a totally different scale.

As the new term began, a group of masked and armed men and women approached from the railway tracks that ran behind the school. They entered the playground, rounded up over 1000 children and adults and herded them at gunpoint to the Sports Hall, a building 10 metres (32 feet) wide and 25 metres (82 feet) long. Here they confiscated cameras and mobile phones, rigged up a series of bombs and booby-traps, and announced that they were Chechen militants.

It was not long before the killing began. As police rushed into the playground to help the few parents and children who had made a desperate escape bid, the terrorists fired from the windows of the Hall. Some witnesses later reported that they then shot several male teachers inside the school. Russian security forces surrounded the building and, for a while, there was a stand-off. At no time did the terrorists seek to negotiate, though President Putin uncharacteristically announced on Russian TV that this was a definite option. The terrorists then passed their demands to the police – they wanted the release of 24 Chechen separatists who had been arrested in June – but followed this up by taking 20 of their male hostages to the second floor of the Hall and executing them.

The heat was intense. The terrorists turned off the water supply, and both children and hostages had to drink their own sweat and urine. When the children cried, their captors frightened them into silence by firing guns in the air. In fear, filth and agony, the hostages spent a second night in the Hall. On the morning of Day 3, the mood changed, and at 1.05 pm violence erupted.

The terrorists gave Russian paramedics permission to collect the corpses that were putrefying in the sun outside the building. As the paramedics did so, two explosions took place in the Hall. Troops ran forward, firing at the windows. Shooting broke out inside the building. Not until the smoke cleared and the surviving terrorists had retreated, was it possible to begin to assess the extent of the carnage. In all 330 adults and children had died.

One of the 330 victims of the massacre at Beslan Middle School Number One, killed when Chechen Separatists seized and held the school for three days in September 2004.

The events of 9/11 marked a new stage in the relationship between the camera and history. Never before had a major historical event received live coverage on this scale. Long before it was clear what was happening, hundreds of millions of onlookers, throughout the planet, were watching it happen. And the images that the world saw on that day were immediate, unedited and uncensored, many of them so horrifying that they have seldom been seen since.

At 8.19 am Eastern District Time, Flight Attendant Betty Ong informed American Airlines that a hijack was in progress on Flight 11 from Boston to Los Angeles. Less than half an hour later, the plane crashed at a speed of 490 mph (788 kph) into the north side of the North Tower of the World Trade Center, New York City. For just 16 minutes it seemed like a terrible accident, but then AA Flight 175 hit the south side of the South Tower, and it became clear that the worst crime ever committed in the United States was taking place. Two more planes had already been reported as having been hijacked – AA Flight 77 (Washington D.C. to Los Angeles) and United Airlines Flight 93 (Newark to San Francisco).

By this time TV and radio networks had live coverage operating. Millions saw the second crash live on TV. Global satellite links were beaming reports and pictures around the world, and on the Internet debate on 9/11 had begun. At 9.36 am AA Flight 77 hit the western wing of the Pentagon, setting fire to the building. All 64 people on board and 125 Pentagon staff were killed. At 9.59 am the South Tower of the WTC collapsed, sending clouds of pulverized concrete and gypsum through the surrounding streets. When the wind eventually blew the dust away, the South Tower was gone.

At 10.00 am, knowing something of the fate of the other three hijacked planes, passengers on board Flight 93 began an heroic struggle to wrestle control of the plane from the terrorists. The

9/11

A gallery of those terrorists held responsible for the hijacking of the four flights on September 11, 2001.

Waleed M. Alsheri

Mohammed Atta

Wail M. Alshehri

Abdulaziz Alomari

Satam M.A. al-Suqami

Ahmed Alnami

Ahmed Ibrahim A. al Haznawi

Ziad Samir al-Jarrah

Saeed Alghamdi

Khalid Almihdar

Majed Moqed

Nawaf Alhazmi

Salem Alhazmi

Hani Hanjour

Marwan Alshehhi

Ahmed Alghamdi

Mohand Alshehri

Hamza Alghamdi

Fayez Rashid
Ahmed Hassan
al-Qadi Banihammad

hijackers retaliated by deliberately crashing the plane into a field southeast of Pittsburgh.

By 10.30 am the North Tower of the WTC had collapsed and the worst of the damage had been done, although it was not until 5.20 pm that the 47-storey 7 World Trade Center building (a smaller, third tower) collapsed. But by now much of the world was in a state of profound shock. As yet no one knew the extent of the carnage, just how many innocent people – passengers, flight crew, office workers, rescue teams, passers-by – had been killed. Nor did they know the identities of most of the victims. Relatives of those who worked at the Pentagon had a little more time to hope desperately for a miracle and fear that they were intimately involved in the tragedy.

The crimes themselves were appalling. One eye-witness of the moments when both Flight 11 and Flight 175 hit the WTC described how the first impact was followed by a deafening silence, then a flood of radio calls asking for information. He was a stonemason, working on outer facing of the 60th storey of the old Pan Am building. "We observe what appeared to be an observer plane coming in for a 'look see'. But suddenly it ploughs into the other tower... explosion... fire ball... that's deliberate... all of a sudden it becomes apparent that we are a potential target... everyone starts yelling 'Get down! Get down!'... Huge hanging rigs and crews drop down the sides of the building in record time..."

It was not until 4.00 pm that the name Osama bin Laden was officially mentioned in connection with the crimes. Earlier President Bush had broadcast to the world saying:

(top) At 9.36 am Flight 77 crashed into the west side of the Pentagon. (opposite) With smoke erupting from its upper floors, the second of the Twin Towers at the World Trade Center starts to collapse, showering glass, concrete, plaster and debris over the streets of downtown New York.

"Freedom itself was attacked this morning by a faceless coward, and freedom will be defended. The United States will hunt down and punish those responsible for these cowardly acts." The hijackers themselves were, of course, already dead, but it was clear that a crime on this scale needed planning, resources and funding way beyond the capabilities of a handful of terrorists.

That night, after addressing the nation on TV, President Bush wrote in his diary: "The Pearl Harbor of the 21st century took place today. We think it's Osama bin Laden…"

(*above*) Rescue workers stand amidst the wreckage of the World Trade Center two days after the terrorist outrage. Inside the ruins are the bodies of many of their colleagues. (*opposite*) One of the many New Yorkers who were caught in the dust storm that followed the collapse of the Twin Towers takes refuge in another office building.

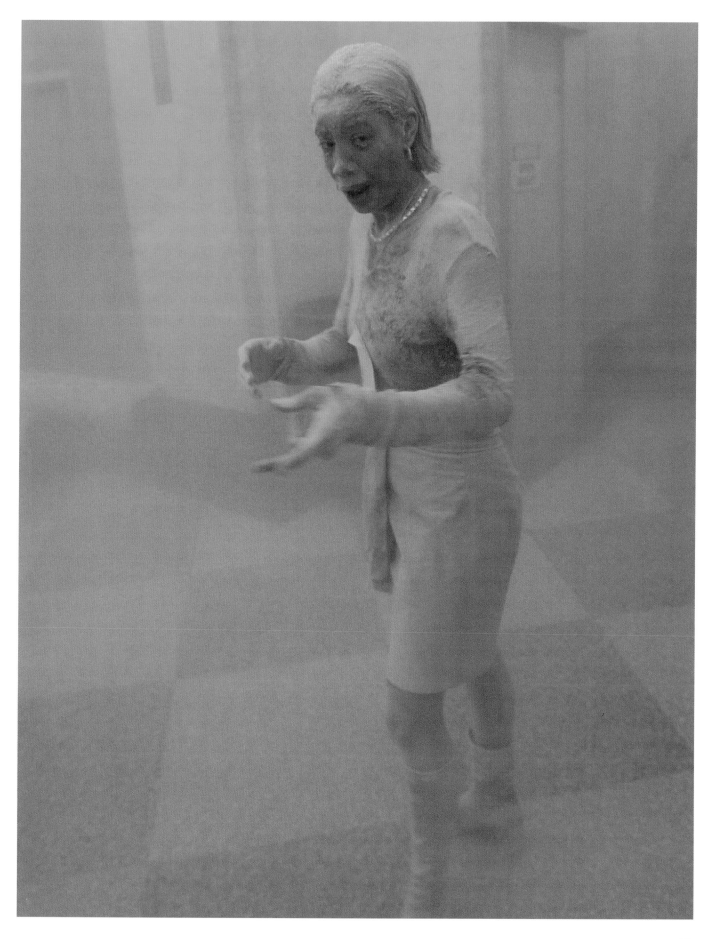

On March 11, 2004, during the early morning rush-hour, a series of bombs detonated on commuter trains in and around three of Madrid's railway stations – the main terminus of Atocha, and two smaller ones, El Pozo and Santa Eugenia. The attacks were co-ordinated, all 10 explosions taking place within a period of three minutes, killing 192 people and injuring over 2000 others. There had been no warning of the attacks, and the slaughter was appalling. Emergency field hospitals were set up. Thousands flocked to hospitals and mobile blood transfusion units. All TV stations replaced their logos with the Spanish flag overlaid with black ribbons. The head of the Catalan government, Juan Maragall, announced "We are all Madrilenos today," and sympathy poured in from around the world.

Significantly, the attacks had taken place just three days before national elections in Spain, which may have influenced the Spanish government in its initial announcement that the Basque separatist group ETA were responsible. This was always unlikely. In the past, ETA had constantly given warnings before detonating bombs, and this horror was on a scale far beyond anything ETA had ever attempted. On the day after the attacks, however, millions of Spanish went on to the streets in government-organized demonstrations against ETA.

Then came reports that those responsible were Islamic militants, headed by Jamal Zougam, Sehrane Abdelmaji and Jamal Ahmida, all of whom killed themselves on April 3, 2004. Other suspects escaped. It was also rumoured that the Spanish government had blamed ETA rather than Islamic extremists, to refute the suggestion that the bombings had anything to do with Spanish involvement in the Iraq war.

Two years later, a group of 29 Moroccan, Syrian and Algerian Muslims were charged with involvement in the Madrid bombings. On October 31, 2007, 28 of the defendants were found guilty on charges ranging from forgery to murder.

Madrid Bombing

Rescue workers near Atocha Station, Madrid, following the explosion that wrecked a commuter train, March 11, 2004.

Serial Killers

Mrs Ann Downey looks out over the Saddleworth moors, England, on October 18, 1965. Police were looking for the body of her daughter, Lesley, who had been killed by the Moors Murderers.

In the 1880s, the East End of London was a tough and desperate place in which to live. It was usual for several families to share one small house or tenement, sleeping on bundles of rags, using an outside lavatory if they were lucky, breathing foul and foetid air, and drinking what could well be contaminated water. Most work was casual – labouring or in the docks – and wages were pitifully low. Life was cheap. Violence and death were regular visitors. A few good souls were pioneering social reform, notably William Bramwell Booth of the Salvation Army and Dr Thomas Barnado with his East End Mission in Stepney, but by and large the East End remained a dark, bleak and sordid place where it was still possible for any would-be pimp to buy a young girl for £5 and set her out on a mercifully short lifetime of prostitution.

Vicious though it was, even this world was shocked by what took place in a small area of Whitechapel and Aldgate between August 31 and November 9, 1888. Five women were knifed to death and their bodies grotesquely mutilated. The first to die was Mary Ann Nichols, a 43-year-old prostitute who had gone out to work on the streets that night to earn the four pence she needed for a bed in a lodging house. Her body was discovered at 3.40 am in Buck's Row (now Durward Street). Just over a week later, the body of Annie Chapman was found near a doorway in Hanbury Street. Her throat had been slashed, her abdomen cut open and her uterus removed. It was estimated that she had been murdered at around 5.30 am, when it was already light.

The press reported the murders in elaborate detail. Fear spread throughout London. The police were much criticized and jeered at for their inefficiency. After the second murder a letter was delivered to the Central News Agency, written in red ink and allegedly sent by the killer known

Jack the Ripper

Mortuary sketch of Catherine Eddowes, one of the Ripper's victims, made on September 30, 1888, by Mr. F. W. Foster.

rom a sketch taken at the Mortuary by Mr F W Foster

.45. A.M. Sunday Septr 30th 1888.

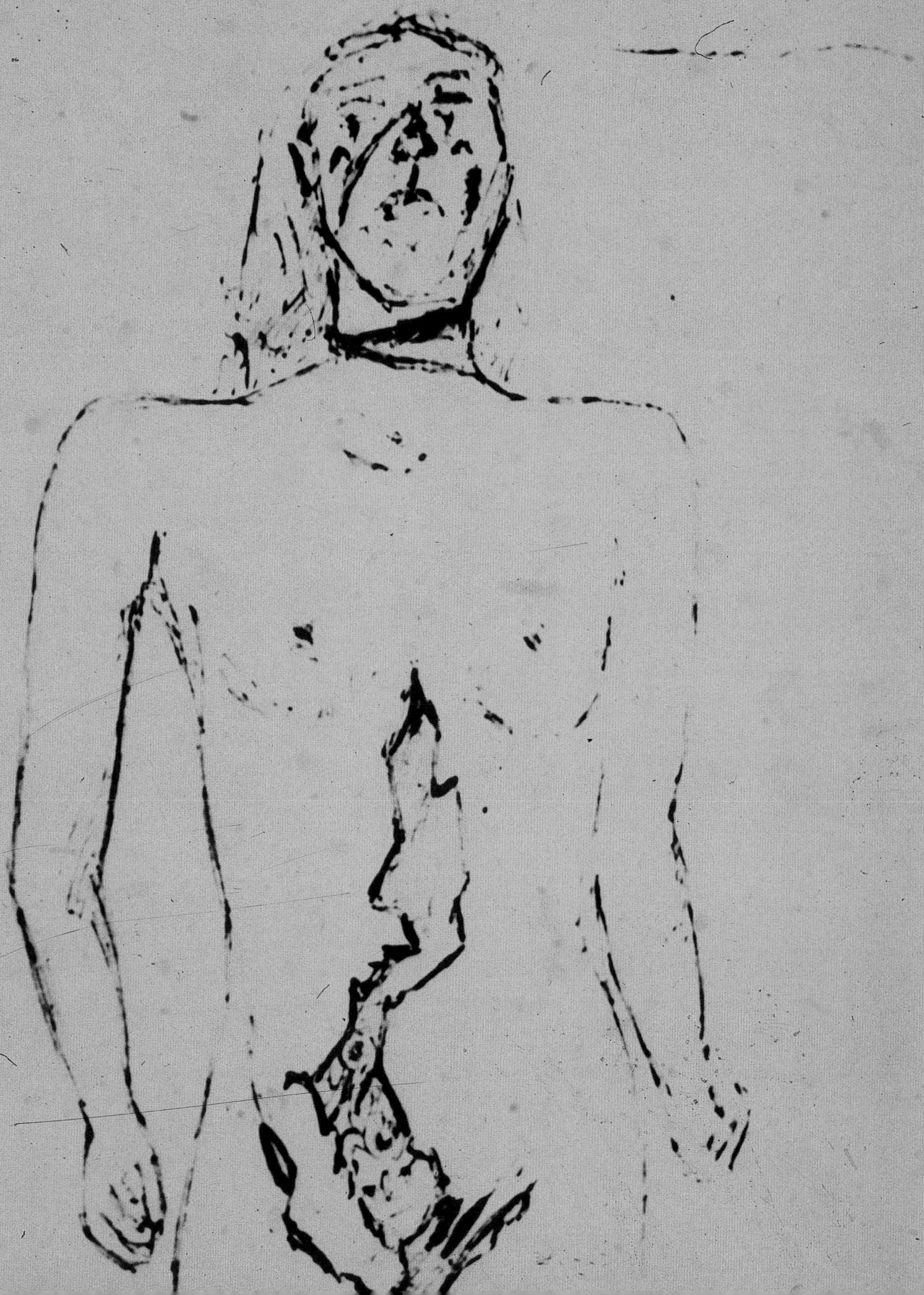

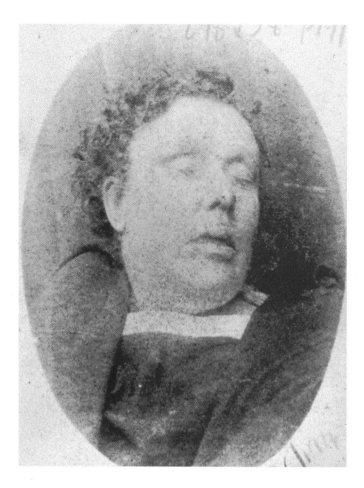

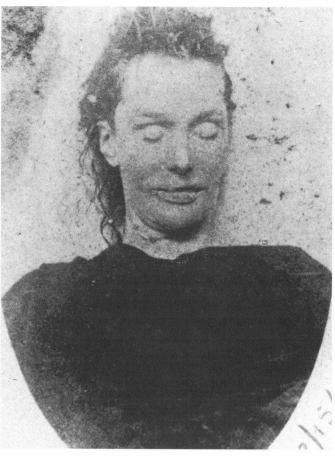

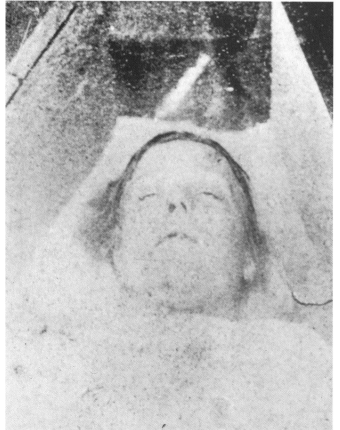

as "Jack the Ripper":

"... I am down on whores and I shan't quit ripping them till I do get buckled. Grand work, the last job was. I gave the lady no time to squeal... I love my work and want to start again. You will soon hear of me and my funny little games...

Good luck,
Yours truly,
JACK THE RIPPER"

Three days later, Elizabeth Stride and Catherine Eddowes were killed on the same night. The steward of a club in Berner Street, Whitechapel, found Stride's body at 1.00 am, lying in Dutfield's Yard. Her throat had been cut but there

(*clockwise from top left*) Annie Chapman, killed in Hanbury Street on September 8, 1888; Elizabeth Stride, killed in Berner Street, September 30, 1888; front page of London newspaper reporting "Ghastly Murder in the East-End"; Mary Ann Nichols, killed in Buck's Row, August 31, 1888.

GHASTLY
MURDER

IN THE EAST-END.

DREADFUL MUTILATION OF A WOMAN.

Capture : Leather Apron

Another murder of a character even more diabolical than that perpetrated in Buck's Row, on Friday week, was discovered in the same neighbourhood, on Saturday morning. At about six o'clock a woman was found lying in a back yard at the foot of a passage leading to a lodging house in a Old Brown's Lane, Spitalfields. The house is occupied by a Mrs. Richardson, who lets it out to lodgers, and the door which admits to this passage, and the foot of which lies the yard where the body was found, is always open for the convenience of lodgers. A lodger named Davis was going down to work at the time mentioned and found the woman lying on her back close to the flight of steps leading into the yard. Her throat was cut in a fearful manner. The woman's body had been completely ripped open and the heart and other organs laying about the place, and portions of the entrails round the victim's neck. An excited crowd gathered in front of Mrs. Richardson's house and also round the mortuary in old Montague Street, whither the body was quickly conveyed. As the body lies in the rough coffin in which it has been placed in the mortuary —the same coffin in which the unfortunate Mrs. Nicholls was first placed—it presents a fearful sight. The body is that of a woman about 45 years of age. The height is exactly five feet. The complexion is fair, with wavy dark brown hair; the eyes are blue, and two of her teeth have been knocked out. The nose is rather large and prominent.

were no other wounds. It is possible that the Ripper's work had been interrupted by the arrival of the steward. Less than three-quarters of an hour later, the body of Eddowes was found in a dark corner of Mitre Square. Her wounds were almost identical to those of Annie Chapman.

The Ripper rapidly passed into folk-lore. The number of his victims was exaggerated – there are still those who say that he murdered 18 women in all and that the killings continued until April 1891. There was wild speculation as to the identity of the man with the leather apron and the bloodstained knife. He was said to be a sailor, a doctor, a priest. Modern analysts have accused Lewis Carroll, Francis Thompson, Walter Sickert, James Maybrick (husband and alleged victim

(*above left*) James Maybrick, a wealthy cotton merchant thought for some time to have been Jack the Ripper – he was poisoned by his wife in 1889. (*above right*) William Withy Gull, royal physician to Queen Victoria and another major suspect in the Ripper case. (*opposite*) Buck's Row in 1888, the scene of the murder of Mary Ann Nichols.

of Florence Maybrick), the abortionist and poisoner Dr T. Neill Cream, and various members of the Royal Family (including Dr William Gull, physician to Queen Victoria) of being the Ripper, but his identity has never been discovered.

Strangely and unintentionally, the Ripper may have done the East End a service. Shortly after the death of Annie Chapman, on September 8, *The Daily Telegraph* published an editorial on "Dark Annie": "Dark Annie's spirit still walks Whitechapel, unavenged by justice… And yet even this forlorn despised citizeness of London cannot be said to have suffered in vain… She has forced innumerable people who never gave a serious thought before to the subject to realize how it is and where it is that our vast floating population – the waifs and strays of our thoroughfares – live and sleep at night and what sort of accommodation our rich and enlightened capital provides for them. After so many Acts of Parliament passed to improve the dwellings of the poor, and so many millions spent by our Board of Works… 'Dark Annie' will effect in one way what fifty Secretaries of State could never accomplish."

The tale of Bluebeard is believed to have been based on the evil deeds of a 15th-century Breton multiple-murderer named Gilles de Rais. The true story of the man who came to be known as "Bluebeard" begins in 1908. In that year, 39-year-old Henri Landru embarked on the scheme that was to result in the deaths of 10 women, one man, and two dogs.

Landru was a swindler and petty crook who had already served several periods in jail. He was a little man, shorter than average, bald, with thick eyebrows that gave him a permanently startled look. He was bright, silver-tongued, callous, romantic and strong-willed. He was also merciless and possessed a sexual appetite said to be ravenous.

He killed primarily for money, and most of his victims were French widows, women who eeked out a lonely and miserable existence in the years of slaughter from 1914 to 1918, or the depressed years that followed. Each killing followed a similar pattern. Landru placed a notice in the Paris newspapers, advertising himself as a "Widower with two children, with comfortable income, serious and moving in good society", who wished to meet a "widow with a view to matrimony". A meeting would then take place, a relationship would flourish, and then the widow would disappear.

His first five victims perished in his villa at Chantilly, and his career as a killer nearly came to an end before it began. He courted a Mme. Cuchet. They fell out, and Mme. Cuchet asked her family to accompany her to Bluebeard's villa to help achieve reconciliation. When they called, Bluebeard was out, and the family found evidence that Bluebeard was a fraud. Nevertheless, Mme. Cuchet and her young son moved in and were never seen again.

Bluebeard

Henri Desire Landru eloquently but ineffectively proclaims his innocence in court, charged with the murders of eleven women, November 1921.

In 1917 Landru moved to a new villa in Gambais, some 40 kilometres (25 miles) west of Paris. Here he installed a large cast-iron oven, and waited two years, before killing again. It was then that Landru's neighbours in Gambais noticed black, noxious smoke pouring from the chimney of the villa. There were at least five more murders here, but in 1919 Landru's luck-of-the-devil ran out.

A Mlle. Lacoste was searching for her missing sister, Mme. Buisson, last known to be living in a villa in Gambais. Mlle. Lacoste found the villa, but it was deserted. The mayor suggested that she contact the family of a Mme. Collomb, who had also disappeared. The hunt was on, and it was not long before Mlle. Lacoste spotted Landru coming out of a shop in the area of Paris where murderer and victim had first lived together. Landru was arrested.

It took two years to bring Landru to court, but when he was tried it took the jury only 25 minutes to find him guilty on 11 counts of murder. He was sentenced to the guillotine, and executed in February 1922. On that last morning he declined to hear Mass and refused the traditional glass of brandy from his jailer. Although he had denied all guilt, 50 years after his death, a written confession was discovered, hidden among drawings he had made while in prison.

Some of the victims of Bluebeard: (*opposite, left to right from top row*): Mlle. Marchadier, Mme. Jaume, Mlle. Babelay, Mme. Cruchet, Mme. Laborde, Mme. Colomb, Mme. Buisson, Mme. Pascal and Mme. Guillin. (*above*) The oven in which Bluebeard was said to have disposed of the bodies of his victims. (*right*) The house in Gambais, where the last of Landru's "wives" were killed.

As a child Peter Kürten suffered dreadful beatings from his father, a brute of a man who was later convicted of committing incest with Peter's 13-year-old sister. In 1892, the nine-year-old Peter was involved in an incident when two young boys drowned in the Rhine, and there is a strong possibility that Peter was responsible for one of the deaths. He was in trouble with the police early in his life and almost certainly killed a 10-year-old girl in Cologne in 1913.

A year later, early in World War I, Kürten deserted from the Kaiser's army. He spent the rest of the war in jail, much of it in solitary confinement, where it is said that he indulged in orgies of destructive fantasy, imagining that he was setting fires or sabotaging railway lines. On his release from jail, Kürten married an ex-prostitute who had herself spent years in prison for shooting a man who jilted her. They made a sad and dangerous couple.

In 1925 they moved to Düsseldorf where Kürten carried out a series of arson attacks and assaults on women. On February 9, 1929, he stabbed a little girl to death – the first of a stream of vicious attacks by the fiend that the press nicknamed the Düsseldorf Vampire. The onslaught continued until May 14, 1930, when he met an unemployed domestic servant named Maria Budlick. He took her to some nearby woods, raped her, and then let her go. Although Maria did not initially wish to report the attack, she later led the police to Kürten's apartment.

He was convicted of nine murders and sentenced to death. Shortly before he was executed by guillotine, Kürten asked the prison psychiatrist if, for a second or two after his head had been severed from his body, he would still be able to hear the blood gushing from his neck. The psychiatrist told him it was possible. Kürten replied: "That would be the pleasure to end all pleasures."

Vampire of Düsseldorf

Peter Kürten, the model for the sadistic killer in Fritz Lang's film *M*.

It is now generally accepted that Marie Besnard was a cold-blooded poisoner. Her guilt, however, was never recognized in court. Her killing spree began shortly after her marriage to Leon Besnard in 1928. Together they formed a plan to kill anyone from whom they hoped to inherit. The first step was to persuade friends and relatives to insert bequests in their wills. Marie had the charm and true dedication to do just this. Next came the killing. Marie's preferred method was poisoning. Over the next 20 years, with Leon's help, she murdered two aunts, several cousins, Leon's sister and father, her own father and an unknown number of friends. Marie then tired of Leon, who had served his purpose in making her rich, so she poisoned him and his mother.

The spate of deaths was noted in Loudun. Neighbours spread rumours as to the origins of Marie's fortune. Her response was personally to visit these neighbours, threatening that something unpleasant would happen if they persisted in their wicked gossip. It was hardly surprising that she was arrested. The bodies of many of her victims were exhumed, and the "Black Widow of Loudun" was charged on 13 counts of murder. But Marie was now a very wealthy woman, with funds to hire the sharpest of lawyers.

By now, forensic science had so refined techniques for the discovery of arsenic in a corpse, that one millionth of a gram could be detected. Sure enough, it was found in the exhumed bodies, but Marie's lawyers cast doubt on the laboratory technique of the prosecution's toxicologists. A second investigation was ordered. Again, arsenic was found, again the defence questioned the technique, pointing out that the radio-active test on the hair of the victims had lasted only 15 hours instead of the required 26. A third investigation failed to convince the jury, and Marie Besnard was acquitted on December 12, 1961.

She was free to enjoy her ill-gotten gains, and the last 19 years of her life.

Black Widow of Loudun

A photograph of Marie Besnard taken during her second trial for the murder of 11 members of her family, March 10, 1954.

As a child, Marcel Petiot was lewd, violent and cruel. He was expelled from one school after another. At the age of 18, he was conscripted into the army and sent to the Western Front, where he was gassed and wounded, and so traumatized that he sought his discharge by shooting himself in the foot.

Hereafter, life improved for Petiot, although the same cannot be said for his acquaintances. He qualified as a doctor, and set up his first practice in a small town near Auxerre. He was known to be a kleptomaniac and when he became mayor, locals were not surprised that money disappeared from the town Treasury. He took one mistress, who disappeared, and another, whose body was discovered after she had been battered to death. The authorities took little notice. Files went missing. Investigations were abandoned. Evidence was ignored.

In January 1933 Petiot moved to Paris, opening a new practice at 66 Rue Caumartin, where he performed abortions and supplied drugs as illicit sidelines. When the Nazis occupied Paris in 1940, Petiot bought another house, at 21 Rue La Sueur and here he started a quite different practice. Posing as a member of the French Resistance, he lured Jews and fugitives to his house with the promise that he could smuggle them out of the country – at a price. They came by the dozen, paid the money and were never seen again. In March 1944, neighbours complained of foul-smelling smoke emanating from his house. Firemen and police entered. In the cellar they found a human arm dangling from a blazing furnace, piles of bones and the remains of dismembered bodies. Scalps and jawbones protruded from heaps of quicklime in the garage.

After the war Petiot was arrested and put on trial. He was sentenced to death for the murder of 26 of the 27 victims whose remains had been found in the underground crematorium and gas chamber at Rue La Sueur, although he may well have killed three times that number.

Dr Petiot

Dr Marcel Petiot, sadistic killer of Jews and refugees in Paris during World War II.

From 1945 to 1949, the German city of Nuremberg was the setting for the Nuremberg War Trials, an unprecedented series of legal trials to establish the guilt or innocence of leading Nazis on a variety of charges. Never before had the vanquished been brought to book following the end of hostilities, and the choice of Nuremberg was deliberate, for the city was seen by the victors in World War II as the site of Nazi triumphalism. There were four main crimes covered at Nuremberg: participating in a common plan or conspiring to commit crimes against peace; planning, initiating and waging wars of aggression; war crimes; and crimes against humanity.

Of the 20 or so principal offenders, 12 were sentenced to death though only 10 were in fact executed. Martin Bormann had been sentenced to death in absentia – his remains were accidentally discovered in Berlin in 1972, and it was presumed that he had been shot by Russian snipers on May 1, 1945. Hermann Göring took his own life by poison on the night before he was due to be executed. Those who were executed included three governors of Nazi-occupied territories in the war (Hans Frank, Alfred Rosenberg and Arthur Seyss-Inquart); two Nazi ministers (Wilhelm Frick and Joachim von Ribbentrop); and two leading commanders of the Wehrmacht (Alfred Jodl and Wilhelm Keitel) – Jodl was posthumously exonerated by a German de-Nazification court in 1953.

Churchill had wanted such men to be refused a trial and to be summarily executed, but the United States rejected such illegalities. Josef Stalin, the leader of the Soviet Union, advocated the mass execution of some 50,000 to 100,000 German staff officers, but both Churchill and Roosevelt would not countenance this. One American proposal was the Morgenthau Plan, a complete de-Nazification of Germany. This was turned down by Stalin. Finally the United States, Britain, France and the Soviet Union agreed on a series of judicial trials.

Nuremberg Trials

Hermann Göring, the Nazi who cheated the hangman, talks to his lawyer, Dr Otto Stahmer, March 23, 1946.

Klaus Barbie joined the Nazi Party in 1932, at the age of 19. Three years later he became a member of the *Schutzstaffel*, the notorious SS. After the fall of France, Barbie was appointed head of the Gestapo in Lyon, in the heart of Vichy France. At first he operated from Hotel Terminus, but after a year moved into new headquarters – complete with specially constructed torture chambers – at the Ecole de Santé Militaire. Here he began his career as "The Butcher of Lyon". No one knows how many innocent people Barbie sent to their deaths in the Nazi concentration camps. It is certain, however, that he was responsible for the brutal murder of 44 children at a farm at Izieu, a few miles east of Lyon.

In June 1943, Barbie's Gestapo agents captured Robert Hardy, an activist in the French Resistance. Hardy was tortured but released, possibly so that he might lead the Gestapo to three founder members of the Conseil National de la Résistance: Jean Moulin, Pierre Brossolette and Charles Delestraint. All three were arrested a fortnight later. Moulin and Brossolette died under torture. Delestraint was sent to Dachau, where he was executed in 1945.

As Allied troops advanced towards Lyon in September 1944, Barbie destroyed all Gestapo records, ordered the killing of hundreds of French civilians who knew about his brutal interrogation methods, and fled to Germany. When the war ended, Barbie was recruited by the U.S. Counter Intelligence Corps. The CIC provided him with a false identity and arranged his passage to Bolivia. Others, with a keener sense of justice, spent the next 36 years hunting for Barbie. In 1983 he was tracked down, extradited by the Bolivian government, and sent to France for trial. Charged in 1987 with the execution or deportation of 842 men, women and children – a small percentage of his victims – Barbie was found guilty on 341 separate charges, and sentenced to life imprisonment. He died of leukaemia in the prison hospital at Lyon in 1991.

Butcher of Lyon

Former SS officer Klaus Barbie reluctantly faces the public outside the Lyon courtroom, May 13, 1987.

John Haigh was a young man with a charming smile and the good looks of a matinee idol. He was also a serial killer with access to an acid bath in a storeroom in Crawley, Sussex, where he carried out his grisly and depraved work. He started with mice, learning that they took only 30 minutes to dissolve completely in sulphuric acid, and worked his way on to larger mammals.

In February 1949 Haigh was living at the Onslow Court Hotel in South Kensington, London. Here he met and befriended Olive Durand-Deacon, a wealthy widow in her late sixties. She mentioned a scheme she had to make artificial fingernails, and Haigh invited her to visit his storeroom where, he said, there might be equipment and substances that could be of relevance. They drove down to Crawley in his car. In the storeroom were gallons of acid and a bath specially treated to withstand corrosive materials. Haigh shot Mrs Durand-Deacon in the back of the neck, stripped her body of anything valuable, and then set about dissolving it in acid, a process that took several days.

As a known friend of Mrs Durand-Deacon he had to report her disappearance – the police were immediately suspicious since Haigh already had a criminal record. They searched the storeroom, and found the murder weapon and a receipt for the victim's coat, which Haigh had taken to a cleaner's in Reigate. More damningly, outside the storeroom they also found fragments of human bone and other remains, later identified as all that was left of Mrs Durand-Deacon.

Having been charged with her murder, Haigh confessed to eight other killings, though only five were eventually attributed to him. He made a desperate and unsuccessful attempt to construct a defence of insanity, claiming that he had killed simply to drink his victims' blood. Evidence that he had killed for financial gain was overwhelming, however, and he was convicted of murder and hanged a month later at Wandsworth Prison.

Acid Bath Murders

In apparently jovial mood, John Haigh arrives at
Horsham Town Hall for his trial, April 1949.

Some 80 years after Jack the Ripper terrorized the East End of London, a killer nicknamed "Jack the Stripper" wreaked the same havoc in West London. Like the Ripper, his victims were prostitutes, though instead of using a knife, the Stripper developed a bizarre form of killing by asphyxiation during deep throat fellatio. And like the Ripper, the Stripper left so little evidence or clues, he was never identified.

There is some difference of opinion as to how many women he killed – some authorities say six, others eight. It is possible that most of the victims knew each other, for several of them were involved in the making of pornographic films. The first was Elizabeth Figg, who was killed near Chiswick on June 17, 1959. Over three years later, the skeleton of Gwynneth Rees was found on a rubbish dump at Mortlake. The last victim was Margaret McGowan, whose body was found behind a car park in Kensington on November 25, 1964, lying in a makeshift grave covered with twigs and two slabs of concrete. It was clear that she had put up a fight to save herself – there was considerable bruising on her neck. It also appeared that her dead body had been kept near a source of heat, for her body was partially cooked, delaying the normal decaying process.

In other cases it appeared that the bodies had been stored somewhere before being taken to the places where they were found. Police began to suspect that this may have been a car repair shed, or a paint workshop, as traces of paint were found on the victims. They eventually found such a place on the Heron Trading estate in Acton, and the main suspect became a 45-year-old man working there as a security guard.

We shall never know, for the man committed suicide and the killings came to an end.

Jack the Stripper

Margaret McGowan, a London prostitute and one of the Stripper's victims. The Stripper was never identified.

On November 17, 1957, Sheriff Arthur Schley and deputies from Plainfield, Wisconsin, arrived at a desolate and dilapidated farmhouse. A local hardware store had been robbed, and the owner of the farm had been seen loitering near the store on the day of the robbery. More worrying was that the storeowner, Bernice Worden, had disappeared, and there had been a spate of such disappearances in Wisconsin over the last 10 years.

Sheriff Schley and his men entered the dark farmhouse and were greeted by the overwhelming stench of decomposition and rotting garbage. As they made their way through the rooms something brushed against the Sheriff's jacket. He looked up to see the headless corpse of Bernice Worden hanging upside down from one of the beams. The search went on and the horrified lawmen discovered that they had walked into a gruesome madness. There were bowls made from the tops of human skulls, lampshades and wastepaper baskets of human skin, a belt made of nipples, a shoebox full of female genitalia, a collection of noses, an armchair, and even an entire suit made of human skin. They also found Mrs Worden's head, in a burlap sack.

It was all the work of a shy, 51-year-old recluse named Ed Gein. As a young boy, Gein had come to Plainfield in 1914 with his parents George and Augusta, and his older brother Henry. His alcoholic father, deemed worthless by Augusta, had died in 1940 and Henry had died in mysterious circumstances four years later. One night there had been a brush fire dangerously close to the Gein farm. After the fire had been extinguished, Ed Gein had contacted the police to tell them that his brother was missing. Henry's bruised body was found on land untouched by the fire, but the county coroner listed asphyxiation as the cause of death.

Gein was now left with his cold, domineering, verbally abusive and fanatically religious mother, whom he worshipped. She had always discouraged him from forming friendships and had

Ed Gein

Ed Gein on the day of his arrest in Plainfield, Wisconsin, November 20, 1957.

ordered him to have nothing to do with women, but a year after Henry's death she died after a series of strokes. Gein was shattered. He boarded off the part of the farmhouse she had lived in, keeping it as a shrine, and inhabited just two rooms on the ground floor. Here he became obsessed with accounts he read of head-hunting, exhumation of the dead and the dissection of the human body. He read obituaries in the local paper, and would then visit the graves of recently buried women to plunder their corpses and peel the skin from their bodies. He later told police he never had intercourse with any of these dead women as "they smelled too bad". A semi-retarded friend named Gus accompanied him on these raids, but Gus was moved to an old people's home. It was then that Gein began killing.

Sheriff Schley's men carried out an exhaustive search of the farm and found the remains of 10 women, but nothing to link Gein to their deaths. After days of interrogation, Gein admitted to shooting Bernice Worden and to only one other murder, that of Mary Hogan, the owner of a Plainfield tavern, who had disappeared three years earlier.

The farm became a "museum for the morbid", with one unscrupulous entrepreneur charging 50 cents per head for a guided tour until it burned down on March 20, 1958. Gein's Ford sedan, in which he transported his grisly souvenirs from graveyard to the farm, was put on display in a

(top) The house of horror where Gein lived. (top right) Police scene-of-crime vehicles at Gein's house, November 1957. (above) Visitors in search of the macabre and grisly peer through the windows of Gein's house. (opposite) Ed Gein's kitchen, where police made some of the worst of their discoveries.

county fair. Children sang songs about Gein, jokes called "Geiners" were bandied about, local people shared what information they had – real or otherwise – with hungry reporters.

As for Gein himself, he was pronounced mentally incompetent, which meant that he could not be tried for first-degree murder. He was committed to the Central State Hospital in Waupan, Wisconsin. Ten years later, he was declared fit to stand trial for the murder of Bernice Worden. He was ultimately found "not guilty" by virtue of insanity and sent back to the Central State Hospital. Here he lived out the rest of his life as a model patient, reading voraciously and playing with his ham radio receiver. He died of cancer on 26 July 1984, and was buried next to his mother in the Plainfield cemetery that he had so often visited.

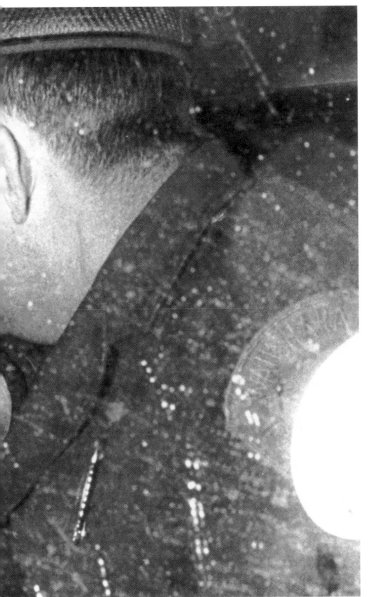

(*opposite and above, left to right*) Earl Kileen, the District Attorney in charge of the Gein case; a neighbouring farmer who employed Gein; Ed Marolla, editor of *The Sun* and a man who investigated the case; Charles Wilson, Head of the Crime Lab; more of Ed Gein's neighbors; the funeral of Bernice Worden. (*left*) The killings come to an end – Ed Gein sits in a police car after his arrest.

They came to represent evil incarnate. A single photograph of Myra Hindley – her hair bleached blonde, her eyes dark and brooding, lower lip pouting, and dressed in such a way that there was an ironic hint of a policewoman's uniform in her costume – remains an icon to many of all that is bad and mad in this world. In Britain, and especially in the area of Lancashire where the awful murders were committed, millions of horrified citizens, lawyers and politicians agreed that the Moors Murderers, especially Hindley, should never be released from prison.

The madness and the badness began in 1961, when Brady's employers recruited a new secretary. Brady was an admirer of the Nazis, Nietzsche and the Marquis de Sade, clever in a sick way and under-educated. Hindley, the new secretary, was putty in his hands and they became lovers. And yet, it was not all one-way traffic. However much she was influenced by him, she also had an influence over him. In some way they were like two awful ingredients in the same poisonous mixture.

The killings began on July 12, 1963, and it was Hindley who lured the first victim into her car as 16-year-old Pauline Read was walking home from a dance in Manchester. Hindley drove the young girl to Saddleworth Moor, on the pretext that she had lost a glove there. She offered Pauline a stack of records if she would help her find it. But it was a pre-arranged appointment with death and Brady, who arrived separately at the Moor on his motorbike. The terrible routine was repeated once every six months over the next two years. Then in October 1965, Brady and Hindley made a mistake. They invited Hindley's brother-in-law, David Smith, to join them. Brady had been grooming him for some months and believed that Smith was ready to commit rape, abuse and murder.

Moors Murderers

Regarded by many as the "faces of true evil": Ian Brady and Myra Hindley pose for police cameras in May 1966.

On the night of October 6, Smith turned up at Brady and Hindley's home to find Brady axeing to death a 17-year-old victim. He was horrified. He did what he could to clear up the mess and hide the body, vowed that he would keep his mouth shut, and then went home and told his wife (Hindley's sister Maureen) what had happened. She persuaded him to call the police.

Six months later, Brady and Hindley were each sentenced to a minimum of 30 years' imprisonment for the murder of five young people. They were denied permission to marry, and over the years in prison mercifully began to turn away from each other. Hindley stopped protesting her innocence in 1986 and died in prison in 2002, having by then served 36 years. Brady repeatedly stated that he did not wish to be released, and that his only wish was to be allowed to die.

Unofficial searches continue for the body of one of the victims, Keith Bennett, but the area of Saddleworth Moor to be covered is immense. Brady's memory of where he and Hindley hid the boy's body is vague, and in July 2009 the Greater Manchester Police announced they were abandoning the search unless and until fresh evidence came to light.

Ian Brady in police custody, October 22, 1965. Unlike Hindley, early in his sentence, Brady admitted his guilt. In prison, the two lovers still wrote to each other for a while, but Brady later broke off the relationship, and subsequently sought permission to starve himself to death.

Between July 1975 and January 1981, 22 women were murdered or maimed in Northern England by a killer who came to be known as the Yorkshire Ripper. The attacks were frenzied and horrendous. In every case the woman was bludgeoned with a hammer and if killed, was then repeatedly stabbed with either a knife or a screwdriver. At first, the victims were prostitutes walking the streets of the red light districts of northern towns. Press and public alike seemed to accept these murders as almost one of the occupational hazards of street-walking, and the police response was routine.

The killings continued but on June 25, 1977, the Ripper killed someone that the press described as an "innocent" woman – a young girl who had only just started her first job in the shoe department of a local supermarket. The search was intensified. There were plenty of clues, for the Ripper was often interrupted in his grisly work. The police knew the killer's blood type, his shoe size, that he had a gap between his front teeth, and had a pretty good idea of the make, model and colour of the car he drove. In the case of his 10th murder, the Ripper gave his victim a brand-new £5 note, subsequently identified as having recently been paid out in wages to Peter Sutcliffe – a man the police had already interviewed in connection with the murders. Indeed, early in the killings, Sutcliffe's best friend strongly suspected he was the Ripper, but could not quite believe that soft-spoken Peter could be capable of such dreadful deeds.

The West Yorkshire Police investigation continued. However, it was handicapped by three problems: the mounting pressure on them to find the killer, especially once the Ripper switched to killing in middle-class areas; their insistent belief in the authenticity of a tape sent in by a character who was dubbed "Wearside Jack", in truth a builder from Newcastle named John Humble who purported to be the Ripper; and the sheer volume of information they had to process –

Yorkshire Ripper

Peter Sutcliffe, the Yorkshire Ripper, is taken into police custody six years after he committed his first killing.

(top) Peter Sutcliffe is covered by a hood as he enters the Dewsbury Court, January 6, 1981. (above) Angry and curious crowds surround the court inside which Sutcliffe is charged with murder. (opposite) The 13 victims: 1. Wilma McCann; 2. Joan Harrison; 3. Emily Jackson; 4. Irene Richardson; 5. Pat Atkinson; 6. Jayne McDonald; 7. Jean Royle; 8. Helen Rytka; 9. Yvonne Pearson; 10. Vera Millward; 11. Jose Whitaker; 12. Barbara Leach; 13. Jacqui Hill. All were prostitutes save Jayne McDonald, Jose Whitaker, Barbara Leach and Jacqui Hill.

12,500 witness statements, 175,000 interviews and five million car registrations. Police computers were in their infancy at the time, generating a great deal of information, but not yet refined enough to process it.

Eventually the Ripper selected one victim too many. Early in January 1981, Sutcliffe picked up a woman and drove to a part of Sheffield frequented by prostitutes and their clients. A police car drove up, making a routine check, and recognized the car registration number. Sutcliffe was taken into custody. The police had no idea he was the Ripper until he calmly confessed to them many hours later.

In 2010, Sutcliffe began the process of asking for release from prison. The High Court of Justice decided on July 16, 2010, that Sutcliffe will never be released.

VICTIM 1
Wilma McCann, 28,
Leeds prostitute

VICTIM 2
Joan Harrison, 26,
Preston prostitute

VICTIM 3
Emily Jackson, 42,
Leeds prostitute

VICTIM 4
Irene Richardson, 28,
Leeds prostitute

VICTIM 5
Pat Atkinson, 33,
Bradford prostitute

VICTIM 6
Jayne McDonald 16,
Leeds shopgirl

VICTIM 7
Jean Royle,
prostitute, 21

VICTIM 8
Helen Rytka
prostitute, 18

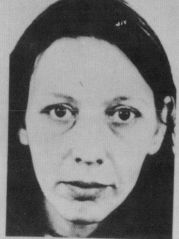

VICTIM 9
Yvonne Pearson, 21,
Bradford prostitute

VICTIM 10
Vera Millward,
prostitute, 40

VICTIM 11
Josie Whitaker, 19,
Halifax clerk

VICTIM 12
Barbara Leach, 20,
Bradford student

Jacqui, the last victim

On the evening of November 14, 1974, police were called to a house in Amityville, Suffolk County, New York. There they discovered six dead bodies – the entire DeFeo family save one. Mother and father, two brothers and two sisters had been shot with a high-powered rifle as they slept in their beds. The only survivor, Ronald Junior (known as Butch), appeared distraught. When questioned, he suggested that the man responsible might be Louis Fatini, a Mafia mobster whom Butch claimed had a grudge against his father.

There were problems with this story. Butch was a hot-tempered young man, a drug addict with a known interest in firearms – he had once turned a loaded shotgun on one of his best friends. More to the point, on more than one occasion he had threatened to kill his father – the last occasion being less than a week before the killings. Although Butch provided a detailed alibi, some of it did not make sense.

Eventually the truth emerged. Early on the morning of November 14, Butch had taken his .35 calibre Martin rifle, gone to his parents' bedroom and fired two shots into his father, two shots into his mother. He had then moved on to his brothers' bedroom and killed both John and Mark with a single shot each. Finally he had entered the room where his sisters slept and killed them.

At his trial a year later, Butch's counsel had attempted to enter a plea of insanity. Butch told the court: "When I get a gun in my hand, there's no doubt in my mind who I am. I am God." There was clear evidence, however, that in the aftermath of the killing he had acted with considerable cunning – throwing his own bloodstained clothes down a storm drain was not considered by the jury to be the action of a madman. He was found guilty and sentenced from 25 years to life on all six counts of murder.

Amityville Horror

The pretty house in which Ronald DeFeo Junior shot six members of his family in a single night. It was subsequently said to be haunted.

For almost exactly a year, from July 1976 to July 1977, the citizens of the Bronx, Queens and Long Island were terrorized by a series of shootings. The victims were almost always couples sitting in a parked car – exceptionally one victim was shot while walking home on her own – and there was no discernible motive in any case. These were random killings and woundings by a madman.

Police Captain Joseph Borelli believed that they were the work of a woman-hater, but a letter found at the scene of an attack in April 1977 denied this. It was from the killer himself, who appeared deeply hurt by Borelli's suggestion. "I am not a woman-hater. But I am a monster. I am the Son of Sam…" A note from the killer to a New York newspaper used the same title, and has gone down in the annals of crime.

The Son of Sam indulged himself in just two more shootings – on June 26 and July 31, 1977. In the first a young couple were both shot and wounded; in the second the woman was killed, the man blinded. But the Son of Sam now made a mistake. When he returned to his own car from the last shooting, he found a parking ticket on the windscreen. A woman walking her dog nearby noticed that he tore up the ticket and threw it away. She also noticed that he had a gun.

The police traced the owner of the car – a young postal-worker named David Berkowitz. He lived on his own in Yonkers and had deep-seated feelings of persecution. Berkowitz was also reckoned to be mentally ill. He claimed that he heard voices of demons telling him to kill. He also said that after killing he felt "flushed with power".

He was, however, judged to be sane and was sentenced to 365 years' imprisonment.

Son of Sam

The police mug shot of David Berkowitz, the New York
City serial killer who called himself "Son of Sam".

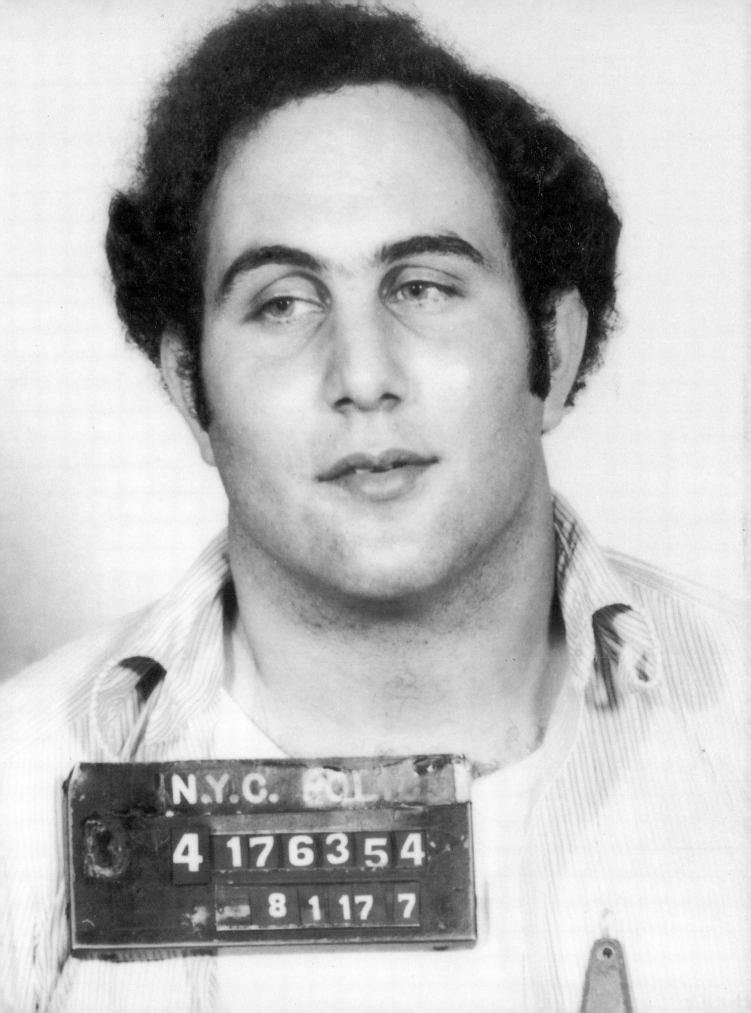

Between November 1 and November 29, 1977, members of the Los Angeles police found the bodies of eight women dumped on kerbsides or hillsides in and around the city. All were between 12 and 28 years old, all had been strangled, some were naked. Another body was discovered on December 13 and two months later the 10th victim of what the press had dubbed the "Hillside Strangler" was found in the boot of a Datsun.

Early in the investigation the police made two important deductions: more than one killer was involved; and whoever was responsible knew the city well. In January 1979 the bodies of two female students were found in an abandoned car near Bellingham. One of them was known to have recently agreed to house-sit for a security guard named Kenneth Bianchi. Bianchi had moved to Bellingham from Los Angeles, where he had lived for a while with his cousin Angelo Buono. Police suspected that the two men were jointly the Hillside Strangler. They were an odd pair. Bianchi was good-looking, while Buono was surly, ignorant and sadistic – he had raped his 14-year-old stepdaughter. The two men had needed money back in 1977, so they had forced two young women into prostitution and bought a list of possible clients from two streetwalkers, Deborah Noble and Yolanda Washington. Yolanda became their first murder victim.

Bianchi made a deal with the state. He would implicate Buono if he could be tried and imprisoned in California – where he would get life, rather than in Washington, where he would be sentenced to death. Once in jail, however, Bianchi changed his mind. In a weird development, a woman named Veronica Compton, who had fallen in love with Bianchi, now agreed to go to Washington and commit a similar murder, thereby casting doubt on Buono and Bianchi's guilt. She failed to kill her intended victim, was arrested and imprisoned. The trials of the two Hillside Stranglers took well over two years. Both were sentenced to life. Buono died in Calipatria State Prison on September 21, 2002.

Hillside Stranglers

The leading figure in a series of horrific murders
during the late 1970s – Kenneth Bianchi,
the Hillside Strangler.

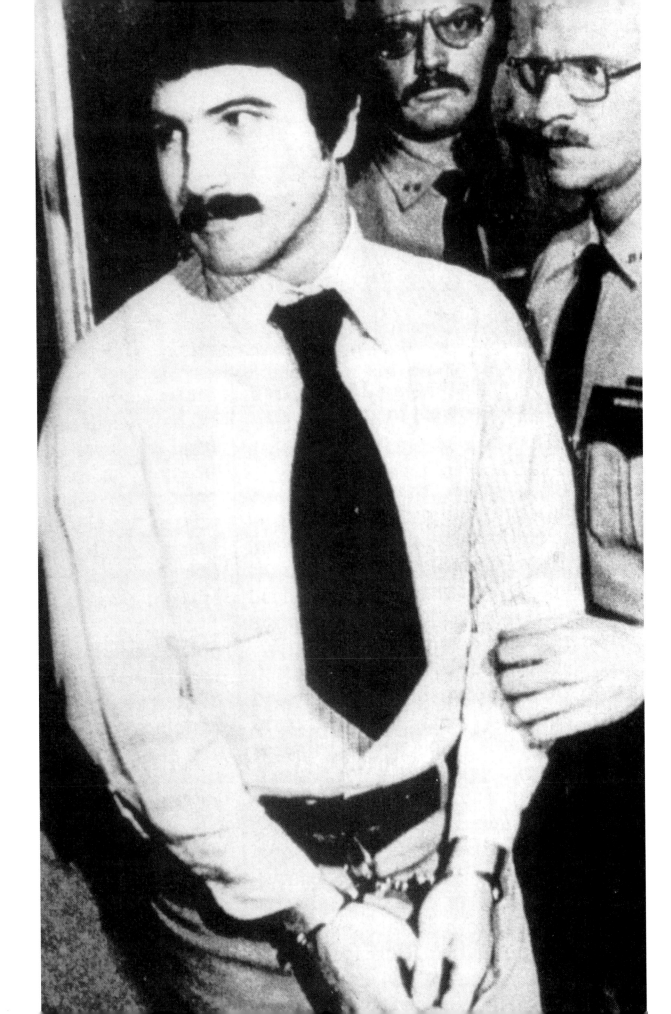

ndrei Chikatilo was born on October 16, 1936, in Yablochnoye, a village in the heart of the Ukraine. It was a tough time in a tough place – an older brother had vanished five years earlier, and Andrei's parents feared that he had been eaten by starving neighbours. Such fears may well have had a profound psychological effect on young Andrei. In 1941 the Nazi invasion of the USSR and the Ukraine led to Andrei's village being overrun by German troops. It is thought that the little boy may well have witnessed appalling atrocities. He was a weak youth, short-sighted, a chronic bedwetter, lonely and painfully shy.

For a while he coped with life – serving in the army, getting a job as a telephone engineer, marrying and raising two children. Then he got a job as a schoolteacher and began to abuse both boys and girls. He was forced to resign, but no other action was taken, so it was not until Andrei was in his early forties that he first killed. This was the dreadful murder of a nine-year-old girl whom Andrei blindfolded, unsuccessfully attempted to rape, stabbed three times, and then, while she was still alive, threw into a bitterly cold river. Andrei was arrested, but was released when his wife provided him with a false alibi.

Three and a half years later he killed again. His victim was a local Rostov girl with a reputation for having "loose morals". He led her to some dense woodland, where he stripped, punched and strangled her, filling her mouth with earth so that she could not scream. This time Andrei was excited by what he had done. A year later he killed again, and then killed six more times in the next 12 months.

A Moscow detective was sent to Rostov to handle the case. It was believed that a single sex-crazed killer, whom they called the Forest Strip killer, was responsible for what now amounted to

Rostov Ripper

30 of the known victims murdered and cannibalized by Andrei Chikatilo between 1978 and 1990.

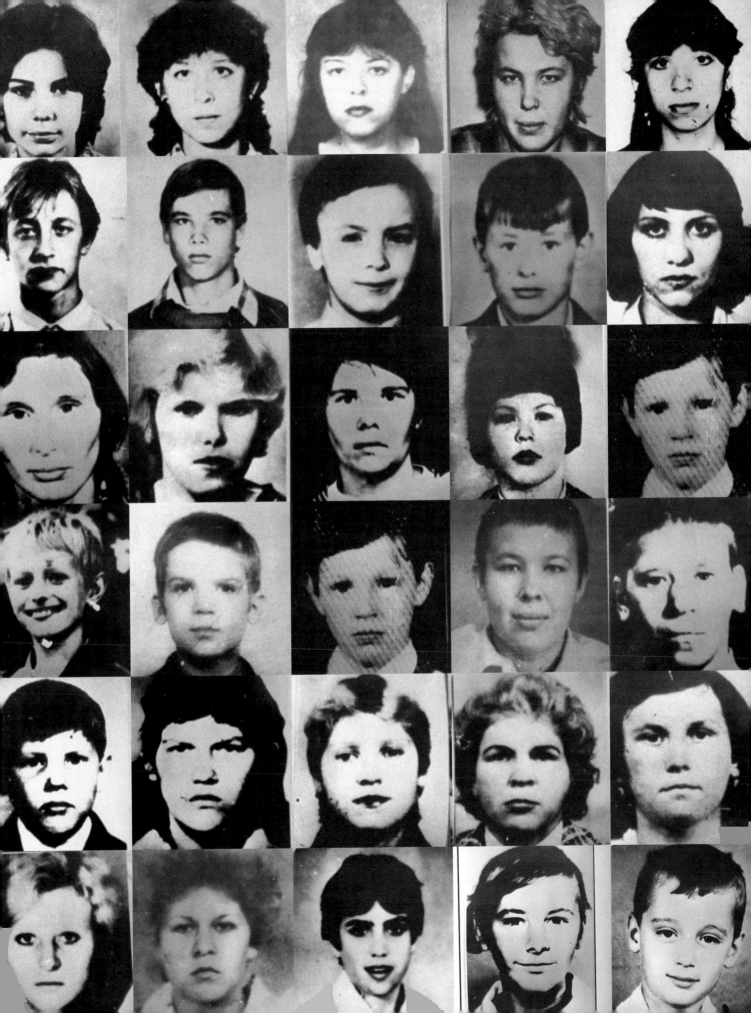

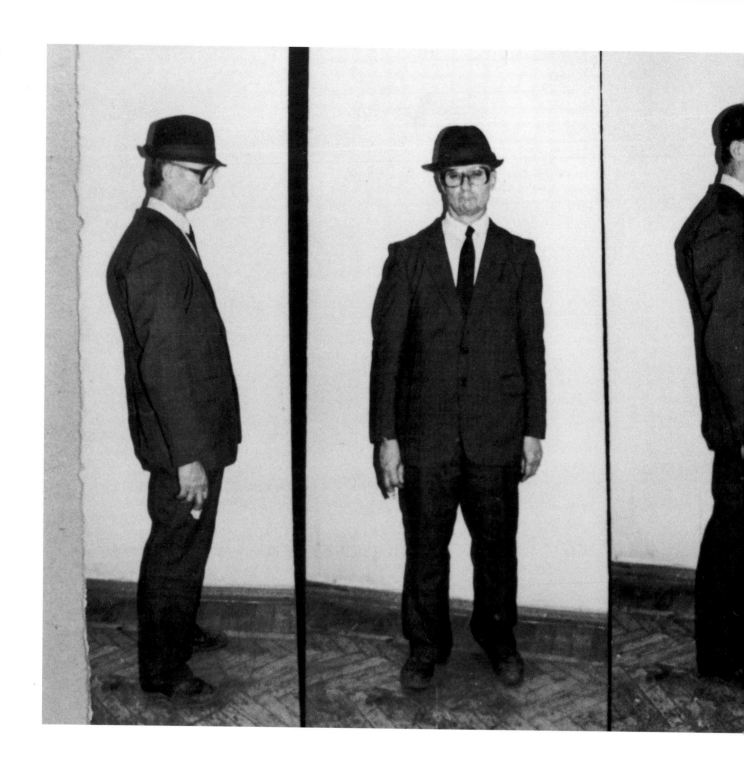

(*top*) Police photographs of Chikatilo taken following his final arrest. (*opposite bottom*) The black leather bag used by Chikatilo to carry the gruesome tools of his trade – a knife, a length of rope and a jar of lubricant. (*opposite top*) The man who tracked down the Rostov Ripper – Homicide Chief Viktor Burakov surveys the mountain of paperwork left in the Ripper's wake.

14 murders, though the term "serial killer" was never used – such a phenomenon existed only in the degenerate, capitalist West. Andrei was suspected and arrested, but released when the results of a DNA test were wrongly interpreted. A year passed, and then a Rostov police inspector saw Andrei hanging around the bus station and approaching young girls. He was arrested on suspicion, but again released. He went on killing.

When he was finally brought to trial in 1992 he was convicted of 52 murders. In 1994 he was executed by a single bullet fired into the back of his head.

On July 22, 1991, two police officers were driving through a run-down area of Milwaukee when they saw a black man with a single handcuff attached to his wrist staggering along the street. He led them to an apartment at 924 North 25th Street belonging to Jeffrey Dahmer, a 31-year-old white. Dahmer opened the door and explained that a bit of drunken foolery had got out of hand. He went to his bedroom to get the key to the handcuffs. One of the officers followed him, and noticed dozens of photographs of dismembered bodies and human skulls inside a refrigerator.

Coming out of the bedroom into the kitchen area, he recognized the same refrigerator, opened it, and screamed. It contained a complete human head. Dahmer was arrested and a thorough search was made of the apartment. The horrified searchers found more human heads, hands and penises in a stockpot, human meat in a freezer, jars of preserved genitalia, chloroform and perhaps the most macabre collection of photographs ever assembled.

Dahmer had killed his first victim while still a student in high school back in 1978 – a young hitch-hiker he had picked up near Akron, Ohio. Over the next nine years he had kept his murderous impulses in check, but in September 1987 he killed again. In his last month of freedom, Dahmer was killing at the rate of one victim a week. By the time he was arrested, he had killed 17 people, all male, all black, all young, all bisexual or homosexual. His method was to invite the victim back to his apartment, give them a spiked drink or chloroform them, then strangle them or stab them to death.

The skulls and preserved items that the police found in his apartment he regarded as "trophies". The flesh in the freezer was meat. The rest of the remains were boiled down with chemicals and

Jeffrey Dahmer

The Milwaukee Cannibal is brought to justice. Jeffrey Dahmer enters the courtroom on August 6, 1991.

Dahmer's neighbour, Mrs Vernell Bass, indicates
the apartment where Dahmer killed and
cannibalized 11 of his victims, July 27, 1991. By
then the refrigerator and freezer had mercifully
been removed.

acids and poured away. The stench from such operations
was overpowering. But Dahmer also performed his own
gruesome experiments. He performed lobotomies on some
of his unconscious victims. In one case he is said to have
drilled a hole in the skull of a man and poured a solution of
hydrochloric acid into it. The poor man lived for several
days in a zombie-like state.

At his trial he was protected by an 18-foot high barrier. His plea of guilty but insane was brushed aside, and he was sentenced to 957 years. He served only two before being murdered by a fellow inmate. To avoid the obscenity of any Dahmer Collection being created, the city of Milwaukee raised $400,000 to buy Dahmer's tools, photographs and refrigerator, all of which were then destroyed.

It took Detective Constable Hazel Savage of the Gloucester Police several months to persuade her senior colleagues that they should obtain a search warrant and dig up the patio to the rear of 25 Cromwell Street, Gloucester, England. DC Savage believed that there they would find the remains of Heather, daughter of the owners, Fred and Rosemary West. The girl had disappeared from Gloucester seven years earlier, after leaving school. According to the Wests, she was in Devon working on a holiday camp, but DC Savage had noticed that Heather's National Insurance number had never been used – the girl had neither sought unemployment pay nor registered for employment.

On February 25, 1994, the police found the first of the victims and Fred West was taken into custody. He admitted killing Heather, but swore that his wife had played no part in the girl's death. After further questioning, he agreed to show police where he had buried two other victims, but said nothing of six more buried under the cellar and bathroom at Cromwell Street.

Eventually he confessed to 12 killings in all – almost certainly an understatement. He had begun killing in 1967 when he murdered Ann McFall, his mistress who was eight months pregnant with his child. She and Fred's first wife – another of his victims – had been dumped in fields near the picturesque village of Much Marcle. The first victim whose death was shared by Fred and Rosemary was another daughter of Fred. Her body was found under a house at 25 Midland Road, Gloucester. The remains of the nine other victims, including Heather, were all recovered from Cromwell Street. They were all girls or young women – hitch-hikers, lodgers, runaways, or just unlucky individuals who blundered into the lives of the predatory Wests. Those that were swiftly killed were the lucky ones. Others suffered appalling sexual abuse from both Fred and Rosemary before being murdered.

Fred and Rosemary West

Police photographs of Fred and Rosemary West, taken on the day of their arrest, November 22, 1995.

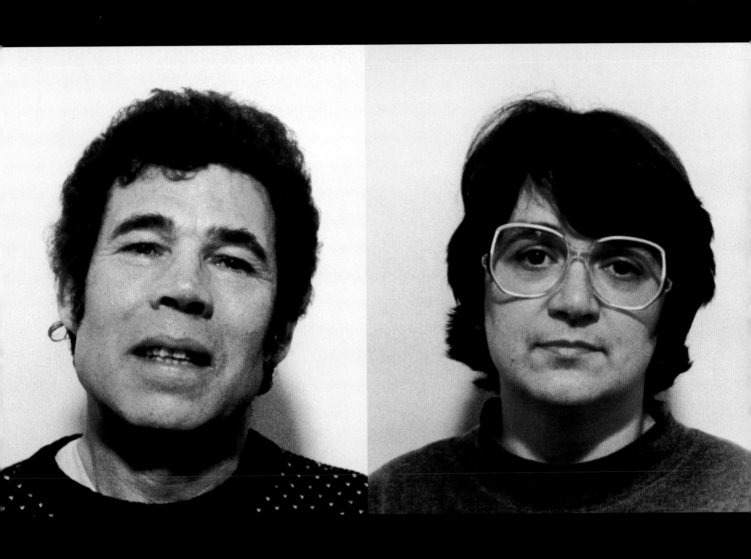

Despite Fred's protestations, the police were certain that Rosemary was his partner in crime. Two months after the discovery of the first bodies, she was arrested and charged with sexual assault. From then on images of the couple, smiling together in the comfort of their cosy home were constantly in the newspapers and on television – monsters of depravity wearing masks of guileless happiness.

On New Year's Day 1995, Fred hanged himself while in Winson Green prison awaiting trial. In October of that year Rosemary West was found guilty on 10 counts of murder and sentenced to life imprisonment. She has since been told that she will never be released. A year later 25 Cromwell Street was demolished.

One of the many boxes of human remains is removed from the house at 25 Cromwell Street, Gloucester, March 4, 1994. After the first body was discovered, it was the eminent pathologist Professor Bernard Knight who identified a third leg bone – the first indication that more than one body had been buried there. The police excavations in the Wests' back garden took months to complete and attracted film and TV crews from all over the world.

Rightly or wrongly, many medical doctors have been suspected of foul play. Their profession gives them frequent and regular access to frail and vulnerable people and supplies them with the means to commit murder, should they be inclined. One doctor who was frequently inclined was Harold Shipman of Todmorden, West Yorkshire and Hyde, Greater Manchester, in England.

A report published by an English High Court judge in January 2005 estimated that Shipman killed at least 250 patients in his 27-year career as a general practitioner. The author of the report, Dame Janet Smith, said: "I think he may well have killed patients late in the evening to avoid being called out in the middle of the night. I think he may well have killed patients who would soon die but who were occupying beds that were urgently needed for other patients. I also think he might well have killed because he was annoyed with a patient or regarded him/her as in some way 'unworthy'." Shipman's own tally far exceeds that of the report. In prison, he confessed to taking 508 lives.

Killing was a way of life for Dr Shipman, who is believed to have committed his first murder within a year of having qualified as a doctor. Certainly by the time he started working in Hyde, at the age of 33, the habit was ingrained. In 1985 police investigated the possible murder of one of his patients, but no action was taken. And so the killing continued until June 1998.

In that month 81-year-old Kathleen Grundy died suddenly. Her daughter went to the police when she discovered that her mother had drawn up a recent will, in which she left all her £350,000 estate to Shipman. Shipman was then charged with the murder of Kathleen Grundy, and over the next three months, the bodies of nine of his patients were exhumed. On January 13, 2004, Shipman was found hanging in his prison cell.

Dr Harold Shipman

A police photo of Dr Harold Shipman. He was aptly nicknamed "Dr Death", though no one knows the number of his victims.

No one, save the killer himself, knows how many people Peter Tobin has murdered. His arrest in September 2006 was for the murder of Angelika Kluk, a 23-year-old Polish student working as a cleaner at St Patrick's Roman Catholic Church in Anderton, Glasgow. In May 2007, Tobin was found guilty and sentenced to a minimum of 21 years' imprisonment. But poor Angelika was only the last of Tobin's victims.

Born in 1946, Tobin was a troublesome child who was sent to an approved school at the age of seven. Between 1969 and 1988, he married three times, each marriage lasting three years or less. In 1991, after the break-up of his third marriage, Tobin moved from Scotland to Margate in south-east England. With him went 15-year-old Vicky Hamilton – alive or dead. In November 2007, her remains were found in the back garden of the Margate house where Tobin had lived. A few days later, the remains of Dinah McNichol were found in the same back garden. Like Hamilton, McNichol had been missing since 1991, when she had been hitchhiking home from a music festival at Liphook, Hampshire. For over 26 years, no one knew what had happened to either of them.

During that time, Tobin moved from Margate to Havant in Hampshire to be near his four-year-old son, a child of his third marriage. While living there, Tobin raped two 14-year-old girls at knife-point, having forced them to drink strong cider and vodka, and then attempted to gas them. He was arrested, pleaded guilty and sentenced to 14 years' imprisonment, of which he served 10 years.

For the murder of Hamilton, Tobin was sentenced in December 2008 to a minimum of 30 years' imprisonment; for McNichol's murder, he was sentenced in December 2009 to life imprisonment. Subsequently, Tobin is reported to have boasted in prison of having killed 48 people in all.

Peter Tobin

Peter Tobin leaves Linlithgow Sheriff Court in handcuffs on November 15, 2007, after appearing in connection with the murder of 15-year-old Vicky Hamilton 16 years earlier. The previous day police had confirmed that the human remains found in a garden once inhabited by Tobin were those of Hamilton.

Assassination

The President of Egypt, Anwar al-Sadat, is assassinated by an armed group of Islamic fundamentalists during a military parade in Cairo on October 6, 1981.

On April 9, 1865, General Robert E. Lee, in immaculate white uniform, surrendered to a mud-spattered General Ulysses S. Grant at Appomattox, Virginia. The War Between the States was finally over, but intense bitterness remained. For President Abraham Lincoln the great task ahead was to bring real peace to a divided nation. On April 14 he made one last speech on the subject of Amnesty and Reconciliation, declaring that the Confederate states should be returned to "their proper practical relation with the Union as quickly as possible". The President then decided to take the evening off and visit a performance of *Our American Cousin* at Ford's Theater in Washington D.C.

Unknown to the President or the authorities, for over three months a group of conspirators had been planning to kidnap Lincoln and hold him hostage against the release of Confederate prisoners of war. Now the war was over, there was no point in kidnapping the President, and the conspirators changed their plan to one of simultaneously murdering Lincoln and members of his cabinet. Their leader, an actor named John Wilkes Booth, visited Ford's Theater on the morning of April 14 and learned of Lincoln's intended visit. The conspirators hurriedly met at a boarding house owned by Mary Surratt and decided that while Booth dealt with Lincoln, George Atzerodt was to kill the Vice-President Andrew Johnson, and Lewis Paine and David Herold would kill the Secretary of State William Seward. The murders were to take place at 10.15 pm.

Lincoln and his wife, with their friends Clara Harris and Henry Rathbone, arrived at Ford's at 8.30 pm. Booth arrived an hour later. He told William Burroughs, a boy who worked at the theatre, to mind his horse in the rear alley and then went to the next-door saloon to fortify himself with a drink. He entered the theatre at 10.07 pm. He knew Ford's well and had no difficulty making his way to the State Box. Here he was in luck. Lincoln's bodyguard, John Parker of the Metropolitan

Lincoln
Assassination

John Wilkes Booth, the man who killed President Abraham Lincoln.

Police Force, had temporarily left his post. Drawing his single shot Derringer and a hunting knife, Booth entered the box, shot Lincoln in the back of the head at point blank range, stabbed Rathbone in the arm, and leapt 11 feet (3.3 metres) to the stage below. As he landed, he broke his left fibula just above the ankle. In front of an audience of more than a 1000 people, while Mrs Lincoln screamed, Booth flashed his knife and shouted "Thus always to tyrants!". He then limped to the back door of the theatre and galloped away on his horse. A doctor in the theatre audience hurried to the President's box. He found that the bullet had entered through Lincoln's left ear and lodged behind his right eye. The President was paralyzed and hardly able to breathe. He never recovered consciousness and died nine hours later, a little before 7.30 in the morning at the Petersen house, opposite the theatre.

Booth rode through the night to Surrattsville. Here he met Herold, and the two rode on to Dr Samuel Mudd's house, where the doctor set and put a splint on Booth's leg. The following afternoon, Booth and Herold left Mudd's house and headed south. Eleven days later, federal authorities caught up with them at a farm near Port Royal, Virginia. Booth shot himself. Herold surrendered. The other

(clockwise from top left) Alexander Gardner's portrait of Lincoln, November 8, 1863. A poster offering $100,000 reward for the capture of Booth. The private box at Ford's Theater at the time of Lincoln's assassination. The conspirators: (right to left) David E. Herold, Michael O'Laughlin, Edman Spangler, Samuel Arnold, George Atzerodt, and Lewis Paine.

A considerable crowd of officials and reporters witness the execution of Mary Surratt (extreme left), Lewis Paine, George Atzerodt and David Herold, four of the conspirators involved in the assassination of President Lincoln, July 7 1865.

conspirators were rounded up and four of them, Herold, Paine, Atzerodt and Mary Surratt were hanged on the gallows at the Old Penitentiary on July 7, 1865.

Booth's aim had been to plunge Washington and the Federal Government into chaos, and thereby rekindle the South's fighting spirit. It was all too late. The South had been brought to its knees. The war was already over, and Booth and his companions did little more than prolong

some of the misery and bitterness of its aftermath. As for
the plot itself, Atzerodt had failed to make any attempt on
the Vice-President's life, and although Paine had twice
slashed Secretary Seward's throat, the poor man was saved
by an iron surgical collar that he was wearing. Although the
capital was stunned and appalled, and Lincoln's death pro-
foundly shocked the nation, business proceeded as usual
under Vice-President Johnson's care.

Just before 10.00 am on Sunday, June 28, 1914, Archduke Franz Ferdinand, heir-apparent to the Austro-Hungarian Empire, arrived in the town of Sarajevo. He had come to the capital of Bosnia–Herzegovina to direct army manoeuvres in the nearby mountains. Accompanied by his pregnant wife, the Archduchess Sophia, Franz Ferdinand was in jovial mood. It was good to get away from the stuffy atmosphere of the Imperial court in Vienna, where his wife was not accorded the respect and honour that he felt was due to her. That was because, although Sophia von Chotkovato came from a noble Bohemian family, she had never been considered a suitable wife for Franz Ferdinand. In Austria, she was not permitted to sit at her husband's side in a royal carriage or in the royal box with him at the Opera. Here in Sarajevo, protocol was different. The Governor, General Oskar Potiorek, had made it clear that the Archduchess would be made most welcome. It would be pleasant for the royal couple to spend the day truly together. They set off, driving through the city in an open car.

The Archduke's good mood lasted precisely 10 minutes. Unknown to Franz Ferdinand and his military escort, nine members of the Narodna Odbrana, a group seeking Bosnian independence, were positioned along the route that the Archduke and Archduchess would take from the railway station to the City Hall, where an official reception awaited them. Long before they reached City Hall, however, an attempt was made to assassinate the Imperial couple. As the car passed Nedeljko Cabrinovic, the young nationalist hurled a grenade.

Accounts differ as to precisely what happened. The official version is that the chauffeur of the royal car saw the missile in mid-air, reacted swiftly, and accelerated. The grenade exploded under the wheels of the following car, seriously wounding two of its occupants. The version given by Borijove Jevtic, another of the conspirators, is that the grenade hit the side of Franz

Franz Ferdinand Assassination

The uniform coat worn by the Archduke Franz Ferdinand on the day of his assassination in Sarajevo, June 28, 1914.

(*far left*) In happier times, Franz Ferdinand and the Archduchess Sophia with their children in 1909. (*left*) The Archduke at his reception in Sarajevo, a short while before he was killed. (*below*) Ferdinand and Sophia shortly after their arrival in Sarajevo, June 28, 1914. (*opposite*) One of Princip's fellow conspirators, Nedeljko Cabrinovic, is arrested after his failed attempt to kill the Archduke.

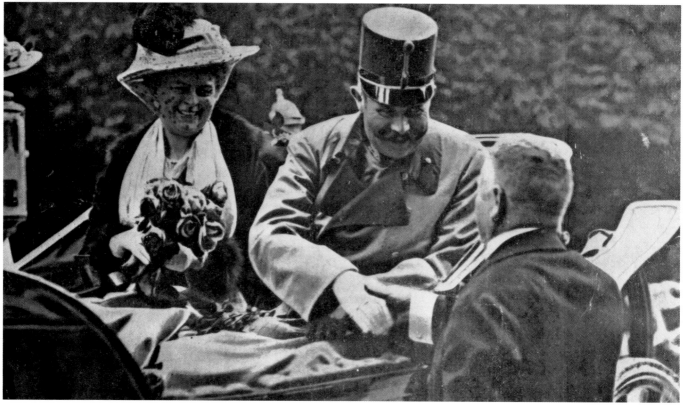

Ferdinand's car, but that the Archduke, with "great presence of mind", threw himself back in the seat and escaped injury. The car drove on at speed to the City Hall.

After attending the reception in the City Hall, Franz Ferdinand asked about the men who had been wounded, and insisted on being taken to see them. A member of the Archduke's staff suggested this might be dangerous, but General Potiorek said: "Do you think Sarajevo is full of assassins?" It was decided that the Archduchess should remain at City Hall, but she refused, saying: "As long as the Archduke shows himself in public today, I shall not leave him."

Unhappily, no one saw fit to inform the chauffeur of the change in plans. He set off expecting to drive to the railway station, not to the hospital. When this became clear, Potiorek shouted to the chauffeur: "What is this? This is the wrong way! We're supposed to take the Appel Quay!" He ordered that the car be turned around. As the poor driver executed a laborious three-point turn, another conspirator, Gavrilo Princip, was passing. He looked up to see the man he and his fellow-conspirators had come to kill sitting in a stationery open car, just a metre or two away from him. Princip drew an automatic pistol from his coat, leapt on to the running board of the car, and fired just two shots.

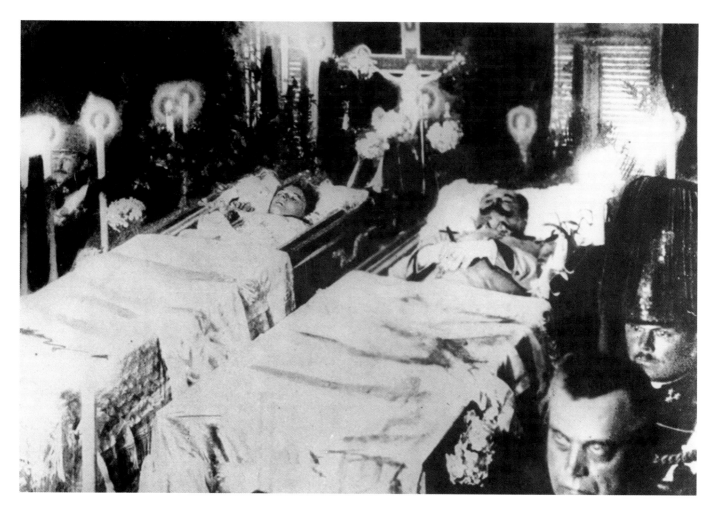

(*clockwise from top*) The bodies of the Archduke and Archduchess lie in state. Members of the Bosnian liberation group attend the trial of the conspirators responsible for the death of Ferdinand and Sophia. The men accused of the murder are brought to court – "1" is Princip, "2" is Danilo Ilitch, and "3" is Cabrinovic. Princip in jail, awaiting trial. Ilitch, seen as the leader of the conspiracy and subsequently hanged by the Austrians.

The first struck the Archduchess in the abdomen. The second hit the Archduke in the neck and pierced his jugular vein. Before losing consciousness, he pleaded "Sophia dear! Don't die! Stay alive for our children!" The car drove off at speed, heading for the Governor's residence. Although both victims were still alive when they got there, they died soon afterwards.

Back at the scene of the crime, Princip had been seized by members of the escort, beaten on the head with the flat of their swords, knocked to the ground and kicked, before being hurried away to spend the rest of his life in prison.

As a direct result of the killings, exactly one month later, Austria declared war on Serbia. The Russian army was mobilized to protect Serbia, and Germany then delivered an ultimatum to Russia. On August 1, Germany declared war on Russia. France mobilized her armies on the same day. Two days later Germany declared war on France and invaded Belgium. As guarantors of Belgian independence, Britain declared war on Germany. Over the next four years, some 15 million men lost their lives in the war that followed, and at the end of it, the Austrian Empire to which poor Franz Ferdinand had been heir, no longer existed.

Alexander Karadordevic was the first King of Yugoslavia, a nation created by the Treaty of Versailles in 1919. By the time he came to the throne in 1929, Alexander had already been King of the Serbs, Croats and Slovenes for eight years. He was King by mischance, for his elder brother, Prince Dorde, had been forced to renounce his royal claims after a series of misdeeds that included kicking one of his servants to death.

Alexander was a soldier by trade, a brave man and a competent general who did much for the Serbian military cause in World War I. He was also a superstitious man. Because three members of his family had been killed on separate Tuesdays, Alexander adopted the practice of refusing to undertake public duties on that day. In 1934, however, on a state visit to France to strengthen an alliance against the newly emerged Nazi Germany, Alexander found himself having to appear in Marseilles with the French Foreign Minister, Louis Barthou, on Tuesday, October 9. As the two men were driven through the streets of the city, their car was attacked by Vlado Chernozemski, one of a group of extremists from the right-wing Internal Macedonian Revolutionary Organization. Chernozemski fired at point blank range, killing Alexander, Barthou, and the chauffeur.

It was the first assassination to be captured by the newsreel camera and filmed in its entirety – both the killing and the aftermath. The poor chauffeur's body became wedged against the automobile's brake, allowing the cameraman to continue filming for several minutes, only an arm's length from the bodies in the car. Chernozemski was immediately cut down by a mounted swordsman, and was then grabbed by the crowd and beaten to death.

King Alexander Assassination

Police surround the body of Vlado Chernozemski, killed by a mob after he assassinated Alexander of Yugoslavia, October 9, 1934.

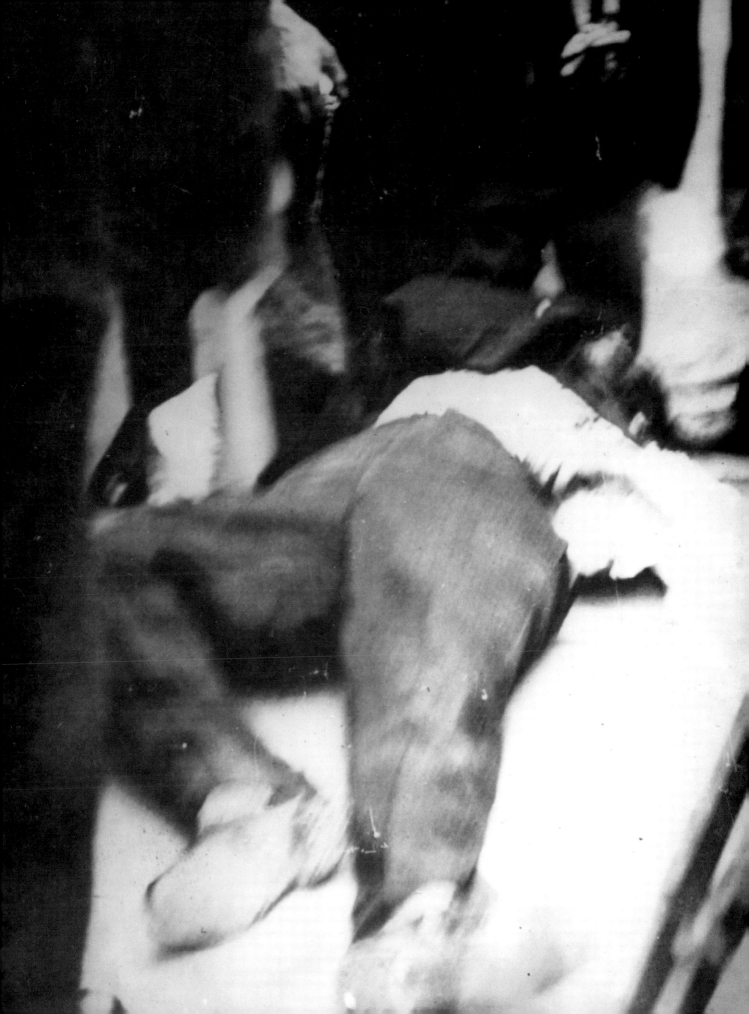

In August 1940 the attention of much of the world was focused on Europe, where World War II was at last in its full horrific glory. Hitler's Luftwaffe were making their daily raids on England. France had already been conquered, the Netherlands overrun, and the battle for North Africa was under way. The assassination of Leon Trotsky was almost sidelined by such events – a grim killing by Stalinist agents, operating far from home in Mexico City.

The row between Stalin and Trotsky had come to a head in late 1926. Stalin, whose own hold on sanity was often precarious, believed that Trotsky had "gone raving mad". Never one to accept opposition, Stalin began to hound all those he called "October leaders", pre-eminently Trotsky, who had to set up an underground press to print his programme for the 1927 Party Congress. On November 7, the last two open demonstrations against Stalin took place. A week later Trotsky and Grigory Zinoviev, another leading Bolshevik, were expelled from the Party. Trotsky was evicted from his apartment in the Kremlin and was finally exiled from the Soviet Union in January 1929.

There were those who wondered why Stalin had not ordered his killing then and there, but Stalin was a cunning man, who knew that Trotsky would act as a figure round which opposition to the Soviet government would rally. Stalin would thus always know where to find his enemies. Trotsky did not have the same comfort. Wherever he went, he could never be sure that an assassin was not lurking in the shadows.

Finally on August 21, 1940, the assassin emerged from the shadows, a man named Mercader who had been a frequent visitor to Trotsky's home. The former lieutenant in the Spanish Republican Army split Trotsky's skull with an ice-axe, piercing the brain of which Trotsky had been so proud. At long last, Stalin was the sole survivor of the old Bolshevik triumvirate.

Trotsky Assassination

Scientists in Mexico City begin their examination of Trotsky's brain following his assassination, August 21, 1940.

By the summer of 1944 it was clear to many high-ranking officers in the Wehrmacht that Germany was in the hands of a madman. Grinding defeats on both the Western and Eastern Fronts seemed not to have registered with Hitler, whose insane optimism was increasingly based on unworkable strategies and phantom armies. While Hitler fumed and sacked his generals, opposition grew within Army High Command. Under the leadership of General Ludwig Beck and Field Marshal Erwin von Witzleben, a plot was hatched to assassinate the Führer.

On the morning of July 20, 1944, Oberst Claus Schenk, Count von Stauffenberg, entered the "Wolf's Lair" – the name given to Hitler's command headquarters at Rastenburg on the Prussian Eastern Front. Hitler was about to hold a conference here with other senior members of the General Staff. Stauffenberg, a war hero and an aristocrat who loathed Hitler, carried a small suitcase which contained a single bomb, one of many British-made bombs taken by the Abwehr, the German intelligence organization. He placed the suitcase under the table at which Hitler would be seated, activated the timer and left the building in haste, heading for Berlin where the plotters intended to seize power in a military coup.

The bomb exploded. Others were killed, but Hitler was only slightly injured. The following day he broadcast to the German people, pointing out that his escape was proof that he was to complete his tasks "under the protection of a divine power". Those responsible for the explosion had no such protection. Von Stauffenberg was captured and immediately shot. Other conspirators had the sense to take the offer of taking their own lives as punishment. Those who were least fortunate were hanged from meat-hooks with piano wire, their executions filmed for the enjoyment of Hitler and senior members of the Nazi Party, and as a warning to other army officers.

Hitler Bomb Plot

Claus Schenk, Count von Stauffenberg, the man who led the assassination attempt on Adolf Hitler.

President John F. Kennedy was shot and killed while travelling in a limousine along Elm Street, Dallas, on the afternoon of November 22, 1963. Three-quarters of an hour after the attack, a man named Lee Harvey Oswald was arrested on a charge of murdering police officer J. D. Tippit. During police interrogation, he was further charged with the assassination of the President. Two days later, while in police custody and on police premises, in front of dozens of reporters and millions watching on live television, Oswald was gunned down and killed by a club owner named Jack Ruby. And that is as much as the world knows for certain about the most famous assassination of the 20th century.

That afternoon, Kennedy's body was flown in Air Force One to Andrews Air Base, and then driven to the Bethesda Naval Hospital in Washington D.C., where the autopsy was performed. Three days later came the funeral – chilling, emotional, reverential, ceremonious. The image of Kennedy's three-year-old son saluting as his father's coffin passed by became an icon of the brief but brilliant Kennedy era.

A week after the killing, Kennedy's successor, President Lyndon Johnson, appointed the Warren Commission to investigate what had happened. Apart from Earl Warren himself, the Commission consisted of six members: one Republican and one Democrat senator, one Democrat and one Republican member of the House of Representatives (the latter being Gerald Ford), a former President of the World Bank, and a former Director of the CIA. Ten months later the Commission issued its report. There had been no conspiracy. Oswald had acted alone, firing three shots from his Mannlicher–Carcano rifle on the sixth floor of the Schoolbook Depository Building. One of these shots had missed the President's limousine altogether. Another had struck Kennedy in the back, passed through his throat and gone on to hit Governor Connally in the back, ending up

JFK Assassination

Robert Kennedy (left), Jacqueline Kennedy and Edward Kennedy stand at the graveside during the funeral of John F. Kennedy, Arlington, Virginia, November 24, 1963.

embedded in the Governor's thigh. This was later to be dubbed the "magic bullet". The third shot had hit Kennedy in the head. The limousine had then been driven at speed to the Parkland Hospital. The President was virtually dead on arrival.

But while the Commission was compiling its report, other versions of what happened were beginning to emerge. It was alleged that Kennedy had been killed on the orders of Mafia boss Carlos Marcello; on the orders of Lyndon Johnson; by disgruntled Cuban ex-pats angry at Kennedy's soft-handed approach to Castro; by the CIA; by agents of the Soviet Union; by the "Umbrella Man" and a dark-complexioned accomplice who were caught on camera at the side of Elm Street as the Presidential motorcade swept by.

Once the Warren Report was published, doubt was also cast on its explanation that Ruby's killing of Oswald had

been a spontaneous act – the motive for which was to spare Jackie Kennedy, the President's widow, the pain of a trial. Firearms experts doubted that Oswald was a good enough marksman to score two hits in three shots fired in six to nine seconds from an elevation of some 60 feet at a moving target. The profusion of such doubts, and the airing of conspiracy theories in a succession of books, films and articles, prompted the appointment in 1976 of a second enquiry – the House Select Committee on Assassinations (HSCA). This second report stated that four shots had been fired (including one from the famous "grassy knoll"), suggested that Ruby had an accomplice in the police who helped him gain access to Oswald, and questioned whether the security arrangements for Kennedy's visit to Dallas had been adequate. The HSCA also noted that in the three years directly following the slaying, 18 material witnesses had died – six by gunfire, three in motor accidents, two by their own hand, one from a cut throat, one from a blow to the

(*opposite*) Bloodstains are visible on the back seat of the convertible in which JFK was shot while riding through Dallas, November 22, 1963. (*above*) New York City commuters read of the tragedy on their way home. (*left*) TV anchorman Walter Cronkite weeps on camera as he announces the President's death, November 22, 1963.

neck, three from heart attacks and two from other natural causes.

More than 40 years on, the world will never know what really happened. What is astonishing is that, at a time when the population of the United States was still reeling with shock and grief, it was possible for so many questions to go unanswered, for so many suspect statements to go unchallenged and for the investigation to wither so quickly. The hurry to get back to business as usual was almost unseemly.

(*above*) Vice President Lyndon B. Johnson takes the presidential oath on board Air Force One just a few hours after JFK's assassination. Events were moving very swiftly. (*right*) The American media identify Lee Harvey Oswald and the gun he is carrying as the man and the weapon responsible for Kennedy's death. (*opposite*) Lee Harvey Oswald's body lies on a stretcher moments after he was killed by Jack Ruby, November 24, 1963.

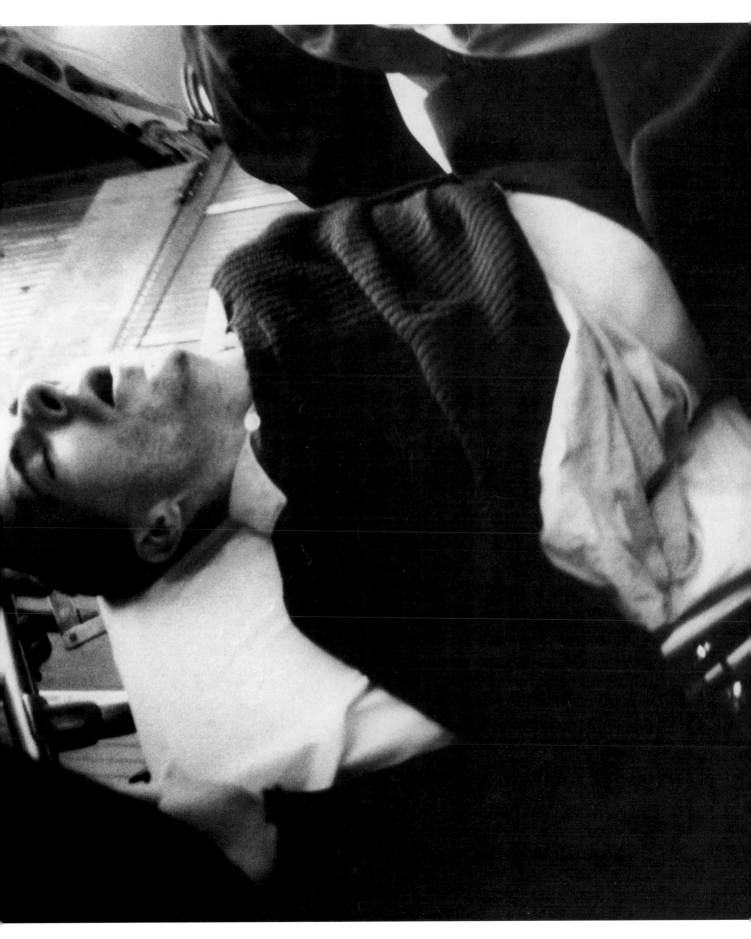

It was the second killing to rock the entire United States within five years. First there was Kennedy in Dallas, then there was the Reverend Martin Luther King Jnr. in Memphis. Two high-powered rifles and a handful of bullets had done their best to wipe out the entire American dream of a new age of life, liberty and the pursuit of happiness.

By 1968 King, in his late thirties, was a man who had realized a great deal of his own personal dream, but the struggle to achieve justice for the black and white alike went on unabated. In March, with the Southern Christian Leadership Conference, King launched the Poor People's Campaign, on behalf of the low-paid and unemployed. On April 3, King delivered his famous "Mountaintop" speech:

"It really doesn't matter what happens now.... some began to... talk about the threats that were out – what would happen to me from some of our sick white brothers.... Like anybody, I would like to live a long life... but I'm not concerned about that now. I just want to do God's will. And He's allowed me to go up to the mountain. And I've looked over, and I've seen the Promised Land. I may not get there with you. But I want you to know tonight, that we, as a people, will get to the Promised Land. And so I'm happy tonight. I'm not worried about anything. I'm not fearing any man. Mine eyes have seen the glory of the coming of the Lord..."

The following evening, King was shot in the throat as he stood on the balcony of his room at the Lorraine Motel in Memphis, Tennessee. The Reverend Jesse Jackson was with him when it happened: "He had just bent over. I reckon if he had been standing up he would not have been hit in the face." A single shot was fired.

Martin Luther King Assassination

A great man laid low... The body of Martin Luther King Junior, April 8, 1968.

Two months later, an escaped convict named James Earl Ray was captured at London's Heathrow Airport. Extradited to Tennessee, Ray subsequently confessed to the killing. But, as in the case of the assassination of JFK, many doubts as to the true killer having been identified remained. Ray had no motive to kill King. He was not a trained marksman. None of Ray's fingerprints were found in the motel room from which the shot was supposed to have come. The bullet that killed King was never matched to Ray's weapon. Witnesses surrounding King at the time of his death said that the shot had come from another location.

The immediate effects of King's death were to make many streets unsafe for white men, to provoke rioting in more than 60 cities, and for a dusk to dawn curfew to be imposed in Memphis itself. The longer term result was for an entire generation to be plunged into a grief from which it never fully recovered.

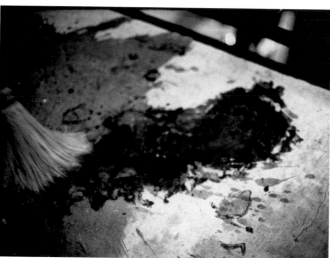

(*above top*) Civil Rights leader Andrew Young (on left) and other witnesses indicate the position of the assassin, Lorraine Motel, April 4, 1968. (*left*) The blood of Martin Luther King Junior on the motel balcony. (*opposite top*) James Earl Ray takes the oath before the Washington committee, August 1968. (*opposite below*) Coretta Scott King at the funeral of her husband, Martin Luther King Jr, April 9, 1968.

At 12.15 am on June 5, 1968 – shortly after winning the California Primary in his presidential campaign – Senator Robert F. Kennedy left the ballroom of the Ambassador Hotel, Los Angeles, to give a press conference. His route took him through a small pantry, and here he was shot. Three bullets hit him, one in the head and two near his right armpit. Minutes later, by coincidence, all three television networks began coverage.

People in the ballroom heard muffled sounds. Kennedy's brother-in-law, Steven Smith, asked everyone to clear the room. Rumours spread that Kennedy had been shot. News reports said he was conscious and had "good colour". Over the next 24 hours Kennedy's Press Secretary Frank Mankiewicz kept the public informed from the Good Samaritan Hospital. Then, early on the morning of June 6, came the news. Kennedy was dead. The young assailant held to be responsible was variously described as being a Filipino, a Mexican, a Jamaican and a Cuban. Eventually he was identified as Sirhan B. Sirhan, a Palestinian whom eyewitnesses reported had shouted "I did it for my country" shortly after the shooting.

The Curse on the Kennedys had struck again, less than five years after the death of JFK. And, as in the Dallas shooting, there were subsequent allegations of conspiracy. A woman in a polka-dot dress and a young man had been seen running from the hotel just after the shooting, crying out "We shot him!" More bullets had been fired than could have come from Sirhan's gun. Evidence disappeared. LA Police Department photographs of the crime scene were destroyed.

Sirhan at first confessed to the crime, but subsequently claimed he was confused by the repeated hypnosis he was given to extract further information. Under Californian law, he was due for release in 1984, but was still in prison in 2006, having been denied parole 13 times.

Killing of Robert Kennedy

Busboy Juan Romero gently raises the head of the dying Robert Kennedy, June 5, 1968.

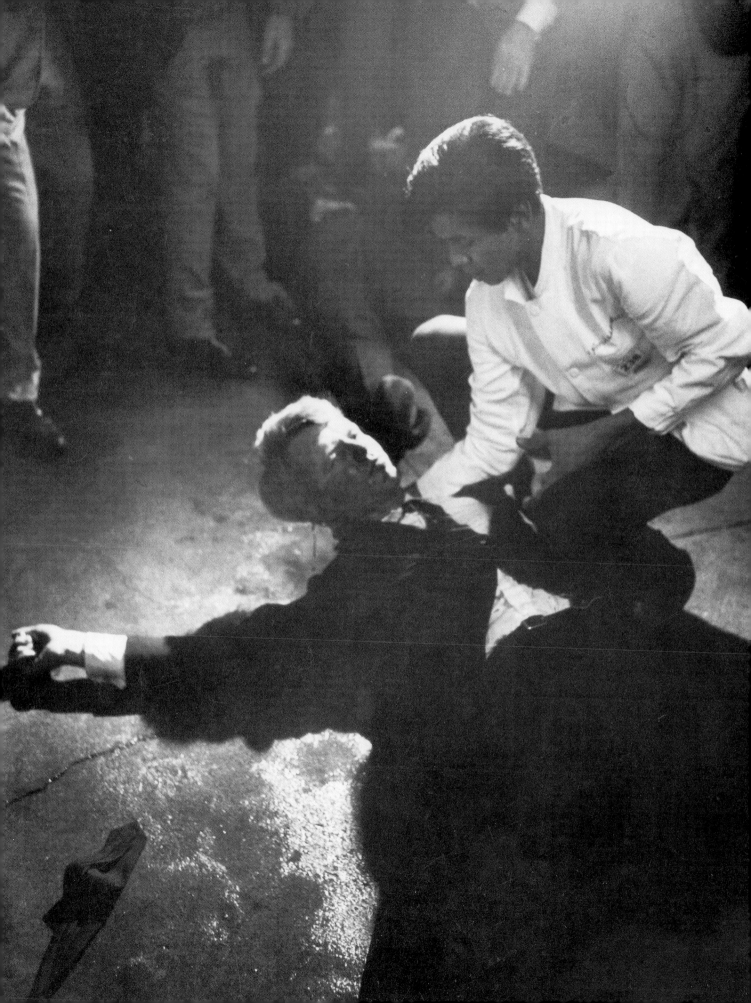

Late in 1980, John Lennon was in New York City, working on a new single. On December 6, Mark David Chapman boarded a plane in Hawaii and took off for New York. What he later described as "a small voice" was telling him to kill the ex-Beatle.

Two days later, at around 5.00 pm, Lennon and his wife Yoko Ono left their apartment in The Dakota at West 72nd Street to go to the Record Plant Studio and work on the new single, *Walking on Thin Ice*. As they did so, several people approached, asking for their autographs. One of them was Mark Chapman, who had with him a copy of Lennon's *Double Fantasy* album and *The Catcher in the Rye* by J. D. Salinger. John and Yoko drove off. Some six hours later they returned. Chapman was waiting for them.

As they walked towards the apartment building, Chapman called out: "Mr Lennon". He then dropped into what the police called "a combat stance" and fired five shots from a Charter Arms .38 calibre revolver. One shot missed, but two hit Lennon in the left side of his back, and two more in his left shoulder. The bullets had been specially filed to inflict maximum injury. Lennon said "I'm hit", and fell on to the sidewalk. He was rushed by the police to the Roosevelt Hospital where he died, having lost 80 per cent of his blood. News of his death was broadcast and a crowd gathered outside The Dakota, burning candles, praying and singing Lennon's songs.

Chapman never denied his crime. He said that he had felt if he shot Lennon he would "become something", that his motive had been envy of Lennon's wealth and fame, and that a "small voice" had told him to "Just do it". He was sentenced to serve 20 years to life and has been denied parole four times, the last in August 2008. Yoko Ono has always opposed Chapman's release.

Killing of John Lennon

Two in a vast crowd of mourners following the death of John Lennon, Central Park, New York City, December 1980.

Four U.S. presidents have been assassinated while in office: Lincoln, Garfield, McKinley and John F. Kennedy. None was killed in the White House or in any of the other presidential abodes. None was killed outside the United States. Only while on public display in their own country have U.S. presidents come to grief.

The last to have suffered a serious attack on his life was Ronald Reagan on March 30, 1981. He was walking to his car from the Washington Hilton Hotel, where he had been addressing a labour convention, when a young man stepped up, confronted the President and fired a series of six shots from a Rohm RG-14 revolver at a distance of 10 feet (3 metres). None of the bullets hit the President directly, but a ricochet pierced his left lung. Ironically, this bullet had bounced off the bullet-proof glass of the presidential car. Three members of the group around Reagan were also hit, most seriously among them his Press Secretary Jim Brady. The assailant was immediately brought to the ground by Secret Service agents. The President was bundled into his car and raced to hospital where he joked with staff in the operating theatre, saying "Please tell me you're Republicans", and said to his wife "Honey, I forgot to duck."

The man responsible was a 25-year-old unemployed depressive named John Warnock Hinckley Jnr. During the five years preceding the assassination attempt, Hinckley had become obsessed with the movie *Taxi Driver* and with the movie actress Jodie Foster, to the extent that he had planned to hijack a plane and publicly commit suicide where she could see him. He then formed a plan to assassinate the U.S. President and thus gain sufficient fame to match hers. Hinckley was not particular as to which president he killed, and prior to the attempt on Reagan's life had spent years stalking his predecessor in office, Jimmy Carter.

Reagan Assassination Attempt

John Hinckley Jnr. is driven from the scene of his attempted assassination of President Ronald Reagan, March 30, 1981.

At his trial on June 21, 1982, Hinckley was found "not guilty" by reason of insanity, although the prosecution had insisted that he was legally sane. The verdict incensed many Americans and four states abolished the insanity defence as a result. Hinckley was confined at St. Elizabeth's Hospital in Washington D.C. After 17 years he was allowed to leave the hospital for limited and supervised visits to his parents. A year later these visits became longer and it was felt that supervision was not required, but the privilege was revoked when it was discovered that Hinckley had smuggled materials about Foster back into the hospital. He remains under close supervision.

The assassination attempt on Ronald Reagan. (*top*) In light rain, Reagan waves to crowds as he leaves the Hilton Hotel. (*above*) Police and Secret Service agents dive to protect the President and overpower Hinckley. (*opposite*) The worst is over, but three victims lie on the sidewalk: Press Secretary James Brady, Agent Timothy McCarthy, and Officer Thomas Delahanty.

In the spring of 1981, Pope John Paul II was at the height of his popularity, respected by politicians and diplomats, loved by Catholics throughout the world, and greeted with joy wherever he went. Nowhere was this more evident than in Rome itself.

On the afternoon of May 13, the Pope was on his way through St Peter's Square in his open "popemobile" when a gunman pushed through the crowd and fired two shots into the Pope's abdomen. At the Gemelli Hospital, sections of the Pope's abdomen were removed during five hours of emergency surgery. A bulletin was then issued stating that "the Pope will recover soon".

The young man who made the attack was Mehmet Ali Agca, an escaped Turkish convict and member of the right-wing nationalist group, Grey Wolves. Agca had sent letters to the Turkish newspaper *Milliyet*, saying that he intended to kill the Pope. When arrested by Italian police, Agca had a note in his pocket saying: "I am killing the Pope as a protest against the imperialism of the Soviet Union and the United States, and against genocide in El Salvador and Afghanistan."

Agca pleaded guilty at his trial in July. His counsel protested that an Italian court had no jurisdiction over a crime committed in the Vatican, but Agca was sentenced to life imprisonment. It was then rumoured that the Bulgarian Secret Service had offered Agca $1.25 million to kill the Pope, and that the Soviet KGB and the Masonic Brotherhood were also involved.

In June 2000 Agca was released from his Italian prison on the orders of the Italian President Carlo Ciampi. Agca had then served 19 years. After serving a further five years for the earlier murder of a left-wing Turkish newspaper editor, Agca was freed on parole in January 2006. The parole was withdrawn soon afterwards. Finally, on January 18, 2010, he was released after nearly 30 years in jail.

John Paul II Assassination Attempt

Bodyguards attempt to comfort Pope John Paul II after the attempt on the Pope's life in St. Peter's Square, May 13, 1981.

The Act of Murder

A man lies in a pool of his own blood. Photographed by
Weegee on January 1, 1939, the victim had been shot dead
after an argument over a game of bowls.

On the night of September 14, 1922, the Reverend Edward Hall, rector of St John's Episcopal Church in the New Jersey town of New Brunswick, arranged to meet Mrs Eleanor Mills, wife of the church's sexton. It turned out to be their last meeting. Thirty-six hours later their bodies were found by another courting couple in the shade of a roadside crab-apple tree.

The affair between rector and sexton's wife was known to others, among them – so the police believed – the rector's wife Frances Hall and her two brothers, Henry and William Stevens. Four years later, Widow Hall and the Stevens boys were brought to trial for the double murder. The motive was convincing enough, but the evidence was extremely weak. Henry Carpender, Frances Hall's cousin was charged with complicity in the murders.

Louise Geist, a former parlour-maid to the Halls, was also called, but then said that she had no evidence to give. Jane Gibson, known in the community as "the Pig Woman", was a neighbour of the Halls. She claimed she had overheard an argument between them, that she had witnessed a struggle, and that this had been followed by a scream and four gunshots. She gave her evidence dramatically, for she suffered from a kidney complaint and addressed the court from a stretcher, while her own mother sat beside her shouting "She's a liar! That's what she's always been!" It was said that the Pig Woman had made up her story for the sake of publicity. For her own part, Frances Hall claimed that at the time of the murders she and her brother William had been in church.

The trial lasted a month, all four accused were acquitted, and since that time no one has admitted to the killings and no names have been put forward as possible killers. The best guess would seem to be that the Reverend Hall and Mrs Mills were murdered by the KKK, as punishment for their sin of adultery.

Crab-Apple Tree Murders

The "Pig Woman" testifies from her bed in court during the Crab-Apple Tree Murder Trial at Somerville, New Jersey, in 1922.

To generations Dr Hawley Harvey Crippen has represented the archetypal domestic murderer. In photographs he appears a seedy little man, meek to the point of creepiness, balding, doleful – the personification of the hen-pecked husband. He came to London from America, and earned a precarious living selling patent medicines, while his domineering and quick-tempered second wife, Cora, pursued an unsuccessful career in opera and music-hall under the name Belle Elmore. Crippen began an affair with his typist, Ethel le Neve.

In January 1910, Crippen bought five grains of hyoscine and soon after, his wife disappeared. At first he told friends that she had gone to America to visit a sick relative. Two months later he said that she had died. Police searched the Crippen house, but found nothing suspicious. Crippen had dissected Cora's body, burnt the bones in a basement fire and buried what remained in the cellar. Frightened by the search, and aware that the police had issued descriptions of them, Crippen and le Neve disguised themselves as father and son, fled to Antwerp and sailed for Montreal on the *SS Montrose*. Their disguises proved totally inadequate. The captain recognized them and sent a wireless message to the ship's home port, Liverpool, the first time radio had been used for police purposes. Chief Inspector Dew of Scotland Yard boarded a faster ship, and arrested Crippen when they reached Canadian waters. The unhappy couple were returned to England.

Tried at the Old Bailey in October 1910, Le Neve was acquitted of being "an accessory after the fact", but Crippen was found guilty of murder. He was hanged at Pentonville Prison, still declaring his love for Ethel, and his innocence. A century later, some forensic scientists have claimed that DNA evidence indicates the remains found in the cellar were not those of Cora, but of a woman who died as a result of an illegal abortion performed by Crippen. In December 2009, the Criminal Cases Review Commission rejected this claim.

Dr Crippen

A detective (second from right) leads Dr Crippen down the gangplank of the *SS Megatic* on the murderer's return to England in August 1910.

On June 17, 1934, William Joseph Vinnicombe, the left luggage attendant at Brighton railway station in Sussex, noticed a foul odour coming from a large trunk. He called Detective Bishop of the Railway Police, who opened the trunk to discover the torso of a naked woman. The following day, the head and legs of the same woman were found in another trunk at King's Cross station, London. A post mortem revealed that the woman had been pregnant.

For the first time in British history, through national and local newspapers, the police appealed to the public for help and information. Lists of missing women were published. Photographs of the trunks were printed. A water diviner offered his psychic skills. But no one came forward to identify the dead woman or to offer information about the trunk. That affair remains a mystery.

However, during the hunt, a local Brighton paper was informed that a prostitute known as Violet Kay was missing, and that at the time of her death she had been an associate of Tony Mancini, lodging at Kemp Street. Mancini was brought in for questioning. There was a problem over his name – he was known as John Notyre as well as Mancini, although his real name was Cecil England. The police then decided to search his house, where they found Violet's body in a black trunk in the cellar. By this time Mancini had fled to London where he was arrested. He told police he found Violet's body in his cellar and had not said anything about it as he already had a criminal record.

He was tried only for the murder of Violet Kay, it being proved that he could not have left the trunks at Brighton station or King's Cross. He was defended by Norman Birkett, one of the greatest defence lawyers in British criminal history, and was acquitted. Over 40 years later, however, he told a Sunday newspaper that he had killed Violet Kay.

Tony Mancini

The bedroom at 47 Kemp Street, Brighton, with the trunk used by Tony Mancini.

Bukhtyar Rustomji Rantanji Hakim came to Edinburgh, Scotland, from India in 1927 to study medicine. He qualified as a doctor, changed his name by deed poll to Buck Ruxton, and took as his common-law wife a Scottish café manager named Isabella Kerr. They moved to Lancaster and had three children, but it was not a happy partnership. Ruxton was a jealous man with a fiery temper, known by servants and the Lancashire police to have threatened to kill his wife on several occasions.

Matters came to a head on September 15, 1935, when Ruxton strangled Isabella. The poor maid, Mary Jane Rogerson, witnessed the murder so Ruxton immediately suffocated her. With both women dead, a cunning calm descended on him. He dismembered the two bodies, removing Isabella's fingertips to prevent identification of the corpse, wrapped the body parts in newspaper, drove 100 miles to Moffat in Scotland, and dumped them in a ravine. He made one fatal mistake, however. The newspaper he used was a special edition of the *Sunday Graphic*, sold only in the Lancaster area.

A fortnight later, two ramblers looked into the ravine and saw what appeared to be a human leg. Police recovered 43 separate pieces of flesh which were passed on to two forensic experts, Professors John Glaister and James Brash. Glaister and Brash matched a finger discovered in the ravine to the prints of Mary Jane that were all over Ruxton's house. They then used forensic anthropology to identify the other victim by superimposing a life-size photo of Isabella's head over an X-ray of one of the skulls from the ravine. The date of the killing was matched to the disappearance of the women by fixing the age of the maggots on their putrefying remains.

Ruxton was arrested, charged, tried and convicted. He was hanged at Strangeways Prison, Manchester, on May 11, 1936.

Dr Buck Ruxton

Dr Buck Ruxton, who once told a police officer: "Sergeant, I feel like murdering two persons... my wife is going out to meet a man."

Weidmann turned to crime early in his life. He was a thief before he had reached his teens, and by his twenties he had left his home town of Frankfurt-am-Main, to become a full-time criminal in Paris. With three other men – Million, Blanc and Frommer – he formed a gang whose aim was to abduct wealthy tourists, take them to a rented villa in Saint Cloud, rob them and dispose of them. It was a plan without finesse, and one that would lead, inevitably, to murder. Their first victim was a dancer named Jean de Koven, visiting France from New York. Weidmann killed her and buried her body in the grounds of the villa. Million's mistress, Collette Tricot, took de Koven's traveller's cheques and cashed them in town.

Two months later, in September 1937, Weidmann killed again. He hired a chauffeur named Joseph Couffy to drive him to the Riviera. When they got there, Weidmann shot Couffy in the head and stole the car. Three more killings followed over the next 12 months, but the police finally tracked Weidmann to his villa from a business card he had left at the office of one of his victims. Weidmann confessed to all his crimes and was tried and convicted in March 1939. He was sentenced to be publicly executed.

The execution took place in front of a large and hysterical crowd outside the prison of Saint-Pierre in Versailles. Weidmann was brought out by warders and marched to the guillotine. He was then strapped to a board that was mechanically lowered so that his neck rested directly beneath the blade of the guillotine. The blade was released, Weidmann's head was severed from his body and fell into the basket placed to receive it, all very satisfactory as far as the due process of law was concerned, but the behaviour of the crowd was scandalous. After receiving a report of the event, French President Albert Lebrun banned all further public executions, though the death penalty was not abolished in France until 1977.

Eugene Weidmann

Eugene Weidmann, thief and murderer, is prepared for the guillotine in the last public execution in France, June 17, 1939.

On the night of August 4, 1952, an English family on holiday camped beneath a mulberry tree on Grande Terre farm, near Digne in Haute-Provence, France. In the morning, the 75-year-old owner of the farm, Gaston Dominici, stopped a passing motorcyclist and told him to fetch the police. When they arrived, they discovered the bodies of the English family. The father and mother had been shot: the little girl had been bludgeoned to death. Within an hour, the police had found the murder weapon – a Rock-Ola American carbine. A splinter of wood from the butt of the rifle was found near the child's head.

So much was straightforward, but over the next three years suspicion fell first on one member of the Dominici family, then another. The most likely culprit was always Gaston, but the problems facing the police and the investigating judge were that he did not seem to have a motive, and he continually changed his story. At one point, Gaston confessed, saying that the killings were an "accident" and had happened simply because he had "touched" the Englishwoman. He soon retracted this confession, saying it had been made under police pressure, and that he had merely been seeking to protect his grandchildren from the horror of the truth. The owner of the gun and the killer was his son, Gustave. The police were doubtful. They already knew that the true owner of the gun was Gaston's other son, Clovis.

The case did not come to trial until November 17, 1954 – well over two years since the killings. On November 28 Gaston Dominici was found guilty and sentenced to death. Gaston then told his lawyer that the killer was his son-in-law, Roger Perrin. The case was reopened, but on February 15, 1956, a final report into the case declared that Gaston was indeed guilty of the murders. In 1957, President Coty commuted Gaston's sentence to hard labour for life. Three years later, President de Gaulle pardoned Gaston and the old man was freed. He died five years later.

Gaston Dominici

The dramatic moment in the little courtroom at Digne, when Clovis Dominici (*left*) accuses his father (*far right*) of murdering the Drummond family, November 1954.

On August 12, 1966, three plain-clothes police officers in an unmarked Q car were carrying a routine stop-and-search operation in Braybrook Street, West London – not far from Wormwood Scrubs Prison. One of the vehicles they stopped was a battered blue Standard Vanguard estate car. Detective Constable David Wombwell and Sergeant Christopher Head walked across to the car to question the occupants. Inside the car were three men who had been involved in an armed robbery – John Whitney, John Duddy and Harry Roberts – and a quantity of hand guns. Guessing that the guns would be discovered, Roberts shot Wombwell, and then shot Head as he ran back towards the Q car. Duddy shot the third policeman, PC Geoffrey Fox.

The three men raced from the scene of the murders, but the number of their car was taken by witnesses – the shooting had taken place in front of passing shoppers and children playing in the street. Whitney, the owner of the car, was the first to be arrested. Duddy was traced to Scotland and caught four days after the killings. Roberts, however, remained at large for three months, while police conducted the biggest manhunt for years. Eventually he was found living rough in Epping Forest, a few miles from the heart of London.

English courts have long dealt severely with anyone guilty of killing a police officer, and, had the crime been committed a year earlier, before the death penalty was abolished, Whitney, Duddy, and Roberts would undoubtedly have been hanged. In fact, Roberts was sent to jail for 30 years.

The years passed. Roberts made several unsuccessful attempts to escape. By 1996 he had served his full initial sentence, but the parole board refused to sanction his release, claiming that Roberts' freedom could have implications for national security, and that there was "secret

Braybrook Street Massacre

The three plain-clothes policemen shot dead within sight
of Wormwood Scrubs Prison on August 12, 1966:
(*top to bottom*) Detective Constable David Wombwell,
Sergeant Christopher Head and PC Geoffrey Fox.

must be kept from Roberts and his lawyer, "special advocate" could consider. In 2001 d that the police were investigating "allega- im, although he was moved to an open

berts was back in a secure prison, accused d in drug dealing and other criminal activi- He was also told that he would not be

released. In 2005 the House of Lords, the highest court in England, reviewed his case. By a majority of three to two, the Lords ruled that Roberts must stay in prison. He has served 43 years. Various reasons are given for his continued imprisonment: that police officers would be incensed if he was released; that government ministers fear a public outcry; that Roberts himself would be in danger. None is convincing, and the mysteries that surround "secret evidence" and "national security" remain.

(*clockwise from top left*) After the shooting one detective lies covered by an eiderdown in the foreground while another lies under the police car. Harry Roberts' hideaway in Matham's Wood, Hertfordshire, near where he was eventually captured after a three-month hunt. A photograph of Harry Roberts issued by Scotland Yard in August 1966 shortly after the Braybrook Street shooting of three detectives.

"It was a disgusting death. I imagined it was a slow death, a death that was shocking, yucky..." Amanda Knox's words describe the murder of Meredith Kercher, a young British exchange student in the Italian university city of Perugia; what makes them particularly chilling is that they were spoken by another young student, on trial for the murder itself. They therefore describe not what Knox imagined, but what she saw.

Amanda Knox comes from Seattle, USA. At the time of the murder she was young, self-assured and attractive, but also what one reporter described as "that most loved of villains – the middle-class monster whose appearance hides a diabolical soul". Knox was certainly unscrupulous. Early in police interrogations, she tried to implicate Patrick Lumumba, her supervisor at a local bar where she worked part-time. Lumumba was entirely innocent and was subsequently exonerated.

If the court decision is correct, and there are some doubts about that, Knox, her boyfriend Raffaele Sollecito, and a local drifter named Rudy Guédé cut Kercher's throat and stabbed her over 40 times. Lurid tales have circulated: that Kercher was at a Halloween party the night before she died, dressed as a vampire and dribbling fake blood, and that the killing was the result of a drug-induced sex orgy that went wrong. The killers attempted to wipe up Kercher's blood with a duvet, and then to clean the apartment with bleach. But when the police arrived at the crime scene on the morning of November 2, 2007, there were bloodstains everywhere.

On the basis of DNA evidence, and the finding of the probable murder weapon in a drawer at Sollecito's apartment, Knox, Sollecito and Guédé were all found guilty of murder. Guédé was sentenced to 16 years' imprisonment, Sollecito to 25 and Knox to 26 years.

On March 22, 2010, the ruling from Guédé's appeal said he carried out the sexual assault on Kercher and then held her down as she was struck with lethal wounds. In November 2010, Knox was indicted on additional charges of slander for claiming that police beat her during questioning. She is set to face trial on May 17, 2011. Appeal hearings for Knox and Sollecito began in Perugia in November too.

Meredith Kercher

"The face of an angel, but the eyes of a killer"... Amanda Knox behind bars in an Italian jail, December 2009. Knox wrote: "It's cold here. I try to cover myself, but I am always shivering... when they let me out in the courtyard I try to stay in the sun as long as possible..."

Crimes of Passion

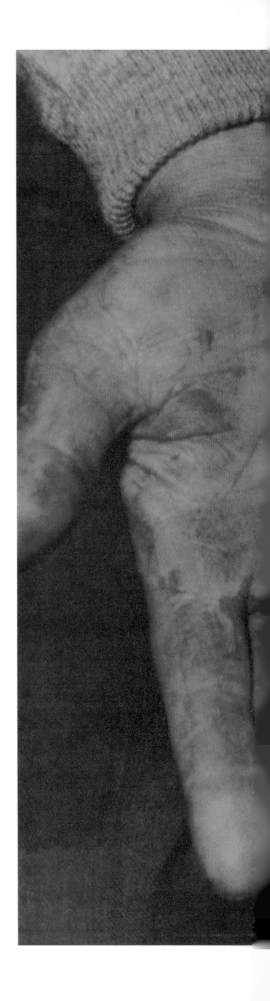

A police shot of the blood-stained hands of Zein Isa on
November 7, 1989. Isa, a Palestinian emigré living in
St. Louis, had stabbed and murdered his daughter,
Tina, after she rebelled against his orders.

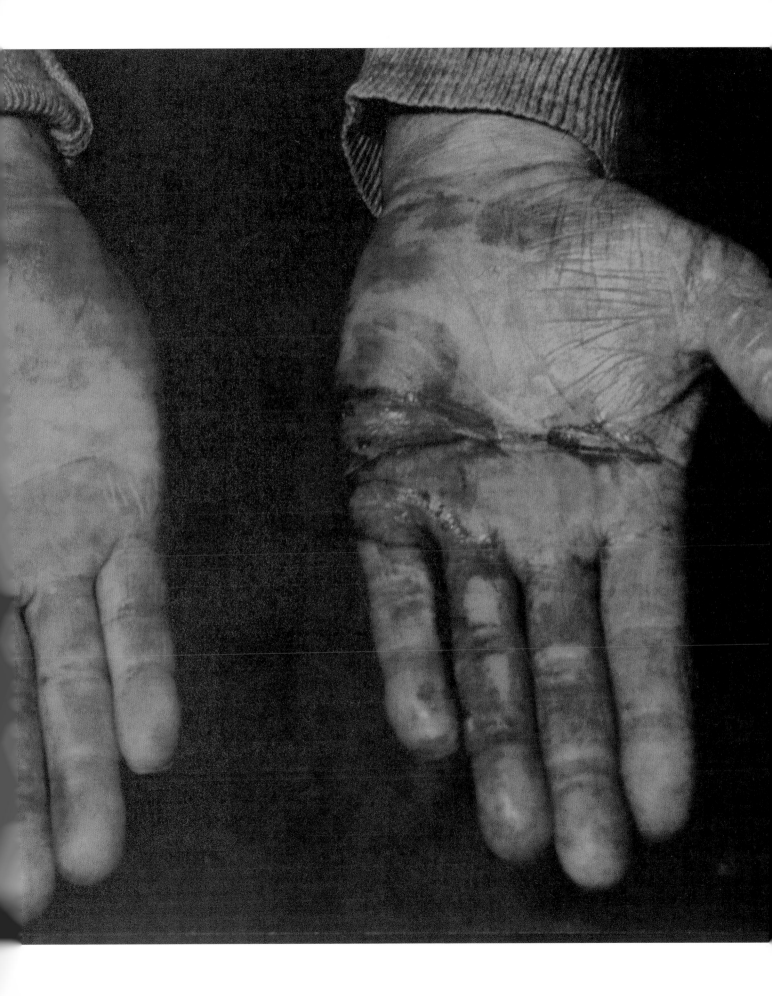

The case of Florence Maybrick has many of the ingredients of a sensational Victorian novel. She and James Maybrick were married in London in the summer of 1881. She was 19, he was 43. She was impetuous and headstrong, but largely an innocent: he was short-tempered, the father of several illegitimate children by his mistress in Whitechapel, and an addict to the heady cocktail of arsenic and strychnine. By 1887, Florence had discovered all these faults in her husband, and had taken on a lover of her own. It was an almost fatal mistake.

Rumours spread. A letter from Florence to her lover was intercepted. Maybrick's brother, Michael, descended upon the household, persuaded James to change his will, and took charge of the estate. Although he had stopped taking arsenic and strychnine, James's condition worsened. Doctors prescribed meat juice. According to Florence, James asked her to add some of "my powder" (the arsenic mixture) to the meat juice. This she did. Forty-eight hours later, he was dead.

Florence Maybrick's trial for the murder of her husband was a travesty. Her barrister was old and inept, and the judge was biased against her. It took the jury only 35 minutes to find her guilty and she was sentenced to death. At the time, there was no Court of Criminal Appeal. Florence Maybrick's one hope was that the Queen herself would intervene, which was unlikely as Victoria was not in the habit of showing mercy to convicted poisoners. However, the public came to Florence's rescue, with a number of petitions for clemency. Her sentence was commuted to 15 years' imprisonment. Michael Maybrick made sure that she never saw her children again.

She died a recluse on October 23, 1941. Fifty years later, a diary was found, which many believe to be that of James Maybrick. If so, it is strong evidence that Florence Maybrick's bad-tempered and violent husband was indeed Jack the Ripper.

Florence Maybrick

Florence Maybrick, who may have killed the man who may have been Jack the Ripper.

In the Paris of *La Belle Epoque* and *Art Nouveau*, of the experiments of the Curies and the last works of Zola, the area of the city known as Belleville was home to gangs of *apaches* – the Mohicans of Paris, men and women who lived passionately and often died the same way. In 1902 one particular story of life in Belleville hit the headlines of almost every French newspaper. At the centre of it was a woman named Amelie Helie, known to the *apaches* as Casque d'Or, by virtue of her stunning hair of red and gold.

Two men fell in love with her – Manda, leader of a group known as *Les Orteaux*, and a Corsican called Leca, who was leader of *Le Popincourt*. The leaders and their gangs took to the streets to settle their rivalry and a pitched battle was fought on the Rue des Haies with guns and knives and little quarter given. The two men were taken to court and when asked by the Public Prosecutor why the battle had taken place, Manda bellowed in reply: "We fought each other, the Corsican and myself, because we love the same girl. We are crazy about her. Don't you know what it is to love a girl?"

Manda and Leca were sentenced to deportation to the island of Saint-Martin-de-Re – Manda for life, Leca for eight years. Deprived of the woman over whom they had fought, their relationship was amicable enough. Back in Paris, Casque d'Or was managing her life perfectly well without either of them, until one of Leca's *Popincourt* brotherhood decided to take revenge on the woman who had ruined his master's life. As Casque d'Or left the establishment where she sang one night, he stabbed her. She survived, but was no longer able to sing. Her career was ruined. As poor Amelie Helie she married an ordinary workman and disappeared from the newspaper headlines, Belleville and the *apache* life. She died in 1933.

Casque d'Or

Amelie Helie, popularly known as Casque d'Or, the
young woman whose beauty caused gang warfare
on the streets of Paris.

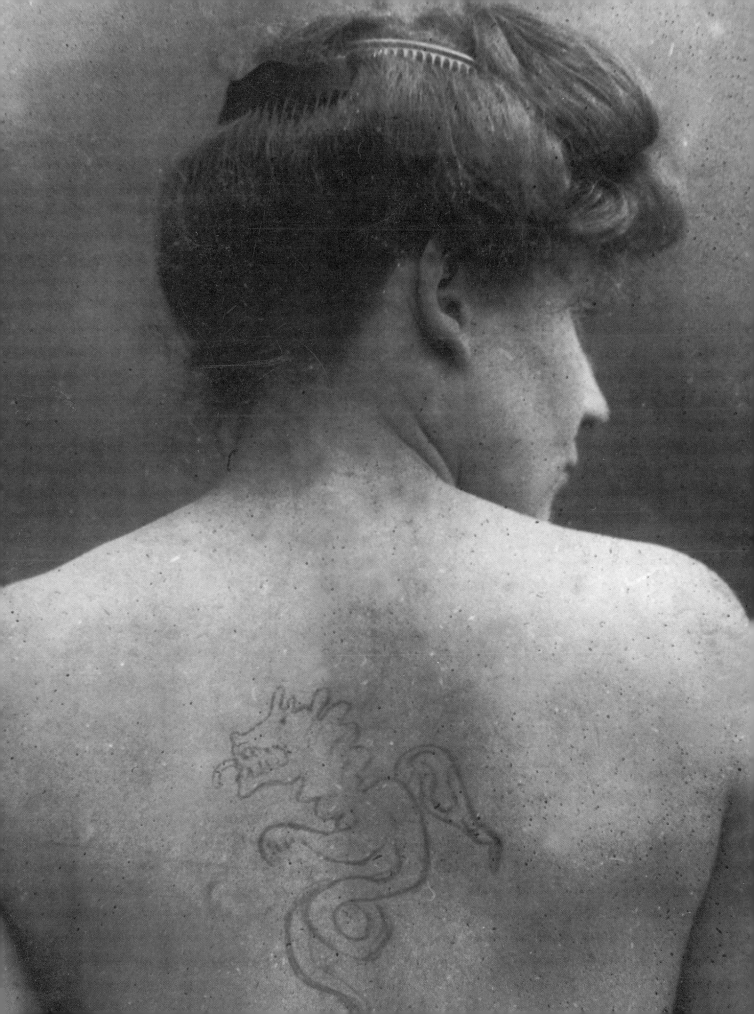

In the late summer of 1907, Count Paul Kamarovsky was shot at his villa near Venice. The killer was a young fellow Russian named Nicolas Naumoff, who was arrested a few days later. A third Russian, a solicitor named Donat Prilukoff, had identified Naumoff as the culprit, but had also hinted that Naumoff was acting for others.

It took three years to bring Naumoff to trial, but as far as press and public were concerned, it was worth the wait. At the trail the Countess Marie Tarnowska – the "Russian vampire" as she was dubbed – emerged as the central figure in a bizarre conspiracy. The Countess admitted having concurrent affairs with Kamarovsky, Naumoff and Prilukoff. Naumoff confessed that he was "infatuated" with the Countess and had killed Kamarovsky out of jealousy. Prilukoff stated: "There was nothing I would not have done at her command. Because she wished it, I left my wife, robbed my clients, sacrificed my honour." He also admitted his part in the conspiracy to kill Kamarovsky.

As the trial proceeded, fierce rows broke out between the Countess, the killer and the solicitor as to who was to blame for the murder. The court held all three guilty in varying degrees. Prilukoff, the sanest member of the trio, was sentenced to 10 years' solitary confinement. Naumoff, a degenerate with "lessened responsibility owing to the fact that he was suffering from mental collapse", was sent to prison for just three years and four months.

Marie Tarnowska, a drug addict who suffered from hysteria and convulsions, was given a sentence of eight years and four months. She was sent to a women's prison in Trani on the shores of the Adriatic, some 50 kilometres (31 miles) from the modern port of Bari. However, she was released after only two years in prison. She did not return to Russia – which was perhaps wise, as the Bolsheviks would have had little time for her – and died in Paris in 1923.

Countess Tarnowska

Countess Tarnowska arrives at the court in Venice to face charges of inciting others to murder, March 19, 1910.

Henriette Caillaux's relationship with her husband Joseph was seldom without incident. They were lovers while he was still married to his first wife, but eventually M. Caillaux obtained a divorce and the couple became respectable. It was as well, for Joseph Caillaux was Minister of Finance in the left-wing government of Jean Jaures, and was coming under heavy attack from right-wing sections of the press, particularly from Gaston Calmette, editor of *Le Figaro*.

Mme. Caillaux believed that her husband should challenge Calmette to a duel. He persuaded her that this would be foolish – one way or another he would be destroyed. So Mme. Caillaux took matters into her own hands. On March 16, 1914, she walked into the offices of *Le Figaro*, saying that she wished to see Calmette. The moment she faced him, she took a pistol from her handbag and fired several shots into the editor's chest, at point blank range. He was killed instantly.

Her trial was a sensation, not only because of the crime itself, but because all France was heavily engaged at the time in what was known as the "woman question". Under the Third Republic a cult of masculinity had grown up, with a fondness for duels and muscular sports. Women were still bound by the patriarchal guidelines of the *Code Napoleon*. It was illegal for women to commit adultery. They could not vote, hold public office, own property if they were married, take a job without their husband's consent. Mme. Caillaux had challenged this man's world.

Nevertheless, it was the old order that saved her at her trial. Her counsel convinced the all-male jury that her killing of Calmette was not premeditated, but a crime of passion, resulting from her uncontrollable feminine emotions. On July 28, 1914, Henriette Caillaux was acquitted. Her trial had been front page news. A few days later it was superceded by a far greater story of male violence – the start of World War I.

Madame Caillaux

Madame Henriette Caillaux, who shot Gaston Calmette, editor of *Le Figaro*, to save her husband's reputation, June 16, 1914.

The case of Yvonne Chevallier contained all the elements of that peculiarly French legal phenomenon – the *crime passionnel*. The victim was handsome, successful Pierre Chevallier, hero of the Resistance in the recent war and recently appointed cabinet minister in the French government. He was also a philanderer, maintaining an affair with vivacious, young Jeanne Perreau – wife of an elderly neighbour. The accused was Yvonne Chevallier, sad and wronged mother of two boys and ill-treated wife of her dashing husband.

In 1951 Yvonne discovered her husband's affair with Mme. Perreau, which was an open secret in both Paris and Orleans, the home town of the Chevalliers. She was shocked and hurt, found it difficult to sleep, and began popping pills and chain-smoking. She made a weak attempt at suicide. Pierre's response was either to deride or ignore her. Finally, in her desperation, Yvonne bought a Mb 7.65mm handgun and 25 rounds of ammunition.

On August 12, 1951, Yvonne made one last attempt to save her marriage. She fell to her knees and begged Pierre to return her love. He contemptuously dismissed her. She produced the gun. He told her to kill herself, but to wait till he had left the room. Downstairs, the maid and the Chevalliers' two sons heard four shots. The older boy ran upstairs. Yvonne took him by the hand and led him back to the maid, saying that nothing had happened. She then returned to Pierre's room, fired a fifth shot into her husband's body as he lay dying, and phoned the police.

Yvonne waited a year in jail for her trial. She conducted herself with dignity and before the trial was over, had the support of the public and the sympathy of both judge and prosecutor. It took the jury only 45 minutes to acquit her. She and her sons then left France for New Guinea, where she died in obscurity in the 1970s.

Yvonne Chevallier

Mme. Yvonne Chevallier gives evidence during her trial for the murder of her husband, November 1952.

If English law had admitted the concept of the *crime passionelle*, Ruth Ellis would not have been hanged. Hers was such a crime to an extreme degree. She shot the man she loved and with whom she had rowed bitterly ever since they met. Each of them was ferociously jealous of the other, violently possessive and fiercely resented the other's alternative lover.

She was born Ruth Nielson in the Welsh seaside town of Rhyl in 1926. At the age of 15 she and her family moved to wartime London. Two years later she gave birth to a son. For a while the Canadian soldier, who was the child's father, visited and paid maintenance, but at the end of the war he returned to Canada. Ruth became a nightclub hostess, married George Ellis – a violent alcoholic – and had another child whom her husband refused to accept as his own. In 1953 she met the man she killed. He was David Blakely, a playboy racing driver with expensive tastes. He loathed Ruth's work and was publicly possessive of her, which threatened her earnings as a club manager. Life became an endless succession of arguments. On April 10, 1955, Ruth shot David outside a pub in Hampstead, wounding a passer-by. She asked witnesses to call the police.

Her trial was a swift affair. It took the jury only 14 minutes to find her guilty. Not until the night before her execution did Ruth admit that it was her other lover who had supplied her with the gun to kill Blakely, and had driven her to the pub at Hampstead. On July 13, a bare three months after the shooting, she was hanged at Holloway Prison.

There was more bitterness in the controversy over the sentence. The *Daily Mirror* columnist Cassandra famously condemned it; 50,000 people signed a petition to the Home Secretary asking for clemency. It was denied. Poor Ruth had timed her killing badly. The murder had occurred during the 1955 General Election, in which the Conservatives successfully campaigned on a pro-death penalty platform.

Ruth Ellis

The sort of image that lost Ruth Ellis public sympathy and subsequently her life, as she models underwear in the early 1950s.

In the summer of 1963, the British establishment was rocked by a scandal of classic proportions, involving call-girls, a Soviet agent, a high-ranking cabinet minister and a society osteopath. Moreover, the settings for this scandal included West End clubs and Cliveden, the Buckinghamshire mansion owned by Lord Astor. The call-girls were Christine Keeler and Mandy Rice-Davies, the agent was Soviet naval attaché Yevgeny Ivanov and the osteopath was Stephen Ward. Ward was a sad character, a man who courted the high life and sought the company of famous people. In so doing, he became involved in organizing high-class prostitution. It was Ward who had introduced both Ivanov and the Tory cabinet minister to Keeler. Subsequently, Ward was put on trial for living off "immoral earnings". On the last day of his trial he committed suicide.

The greater shame and the most glaring publicity were reserved, however, for the minister. John Profumo was a Conservative MP and Secretary of State for War in Harold Macmillan's government. Early in 1963, he assured the House of Commons that there had been no impropriety in his relationship with Keeler. Ten weeks later, he admitted to the House that this had been a lie. Once he admitted sleeping with Keeler, it wasn't long before suggestions were made that he may well have leaked defence secrets to her, and that she might have passed them on to Ivanov. Lying to the House was considered an unforgivable trespass. Profumo was forced to resign and a few months later, partly as a result of the fall-out from this scandal, Macmillan and the Conservatives were defeated in the General Election by Harold Wilson and the Labour Party.

In its own way, the Profumo Affair marked the beginning of the Swinging Sixties in Britain – a time when ancient standards and old rules were called into question, and when the British Establishment lost its hitherto ingrained and automatic respect. The traditional "elders" and "betters" had been shown in a tawdry and unflattering light, and the press made much of the almost

Profumo Affair

27 years after the *cause célèbre*, Christine Keeler recreates her most famous portrait from the Profumo Scandal of 1963.

flagrant honesty of both Christine Keeler and Mandy Rice-Davies, who brought a breath of robustly fresh air to the court proceedings.

Quite how far Ward's circle of acquaintances spread was never revealed, but in her 2001 autobiography *The Truth At Last*, Keeler alleged that Ward was indeed running a spy ring for the Soviets, and that his agents included Sir Roger Hollis, then Head of MI5, and Sir Anthony Blunt, surveyor of the Queen's Pictures. Following a stroke, Profumo died on March 10, 2006.

Three of the key players in the affair: (*above, left*) Mandy Rice-Davies arrives at court, enjoying every moment of her time in the limelight; (*above*) Stephen Ward, the sinister osteopath at the centre of the affair; and (*left*) Christine Keeler – model, showgirl, call-girl and innocent destroyer of political careers. (*right*) John Profumo, Conservative MP and War Minister in Harold Macmillan's government.

On July 15, 1997, Gianni Versace, founder of one of the most famous and successful fashion houses in the world, was gunned down, execution-style, by a young man dressed in slacks, a white shirt, a white cap, and wearing a backpack. It was early morning and Versace was leaving his Miami Beach mansion to make his way to the beach. He was wearing sandals, a dark coloured shirt and shorts with $1,200 in the pocket. None of the money was stolen. Police quickly identified 27-year-old Andrew Cunanan as the sole person responsible for the homicide, although they were hesitant to reveal what motive lay behind the crime.

Later, police announced that Cunanan was suspected of five other murders, which gave a Versace family spokesman the opportunity to state that Versace had been the victim of a maniacal serial killer, and that the motive for the murder was simply madness. Others disagreed, for Cunanan was known to be homosexual and there was evidence that he had met Versace seven years earlier at a costume show in San Francisco, when Versace had approached the young man and said: "I recognize you; where have we known each other from?" There may well have been a mutual attraction. There seems little doubt that Cunanan had become obsessed with Versace, and had been stalking him for five weeks prior to the killing. Some commentators have pointed to the fact that the beach towards which Versace was heading was a meeting place for gays, in-line skaters and, in the words of *Time* magazine, "muscle guys with deltoids like the gas tanks on a Harley".

One week later, Cunanan committed suicide on a houseboat some two miles from the Versace mansion, the scene of the killing. The houseboat mysteriously sank not long after, conveniently destroying any evidence that may have existed on it as to what the real connection was between the fashion billionaire and the backpacker.

Versace Killing

Killer and victim on the cover of *Time* magazine, July 28, 1997. The inset image is of Andrew Cunanan.

TIME

In the Path of A Killer

Gianni Versace
and alleged
serial murderer
Andrew Cunanan

30>

10090

0 724404 1

Kidnappings

Patty Hearst (second from right) is led away from 1827
Golden Gate, San Francisco, by a U.S. Marshal shortly
after her release from captivity on February 16, 1976.

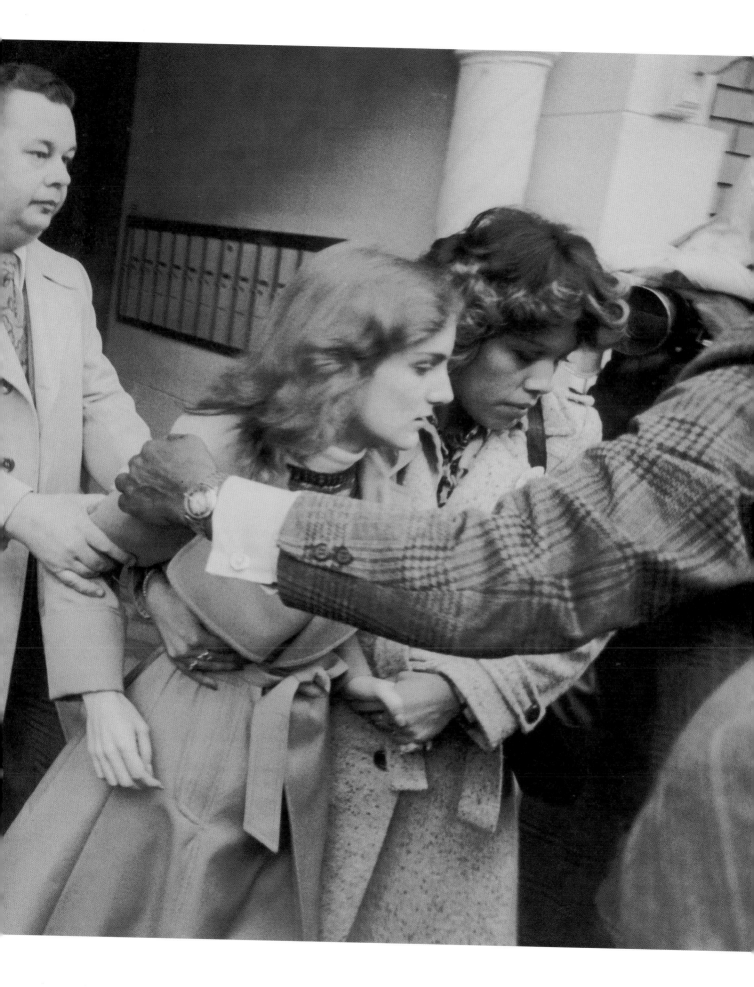

Paris in the late 1920s was a city of glamour, of cabaret stars such as Mistinguett and Sasha Guitry, of the Surrealists and pleasure seekers. It was also home to many White Russian *émigrés* and contained both the court-in-exile of Grand Prince Nicolai Nikolayevich and the headquarters of the anti-Soviet Russian All-Military Union (ROVS). This group of ex-Tsarist officers lived for the overthrow of Stalin and the restoration of the Romanov monarchy. It was a grand dream, toasted nightly in champagne, but it had not the slightest chance of success.

On January 26, 1930, a White Russian émigré named Alexander Kutepov was snatched from the streets of the city. The kidnapping was swift and efficient and Kutepov's disappearance remained a complete mystery. The police had no leads, the kidnappers left no clues. The most likely explanation was that he had been taken by Soviet agents. Kutepov was no friend of the Soviet Union, having been a corps commander in Denikin's army during the Russian Civil War of 1918 to 1920. With the war lost, Kutepov had made his way to Paris, where he became a leader of the ROVS. With him came Nikolai Skoblin, another ex-cavalry officer from the White Russian army. Skoblin was a cruel man with a penchant for intrigue, working as a double-agent – serving the old cause, but also serving OGPU, the Soviet Secret Police. As the years went by, Skoblin extended his activities, becoming a triple agent, working for ROVS, OGPU and the Gestapo.

It now seems certain that Skoblin was at the centre of the kidnapping, that Kutepov was smuggled across Europe, and that he died on the way to Novorossiysk, a prison on the shores of the Black Sea. The dreams of the ex-Tsarist officers came to nothing. The fate of Skoblin remains unknown – some say he was killed in a German air raid on Barcelona in 1938, others that he was murdered by a Soviet agent.

General Kutepov

Kardec, a blindfolded spiritualist, helps Detective Ashelbe (left) in the hunt for kidnap victim Alexander Kutepov.

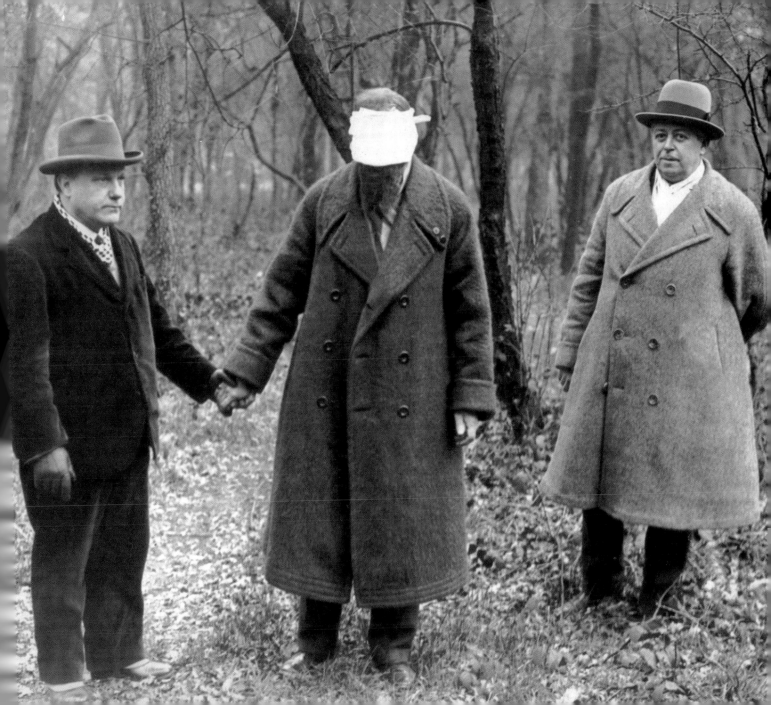

In 1927 Charles A. Lindbergh became a national hero in the United States. At the age of 25, he had been the first person to make a solo flight across the Atlantic. "The Lone Eagle", as the press dubbed him, was modest, charming, and good-looking and his fame lasted. Three years later, he and his wife Anne Morrow Lindbergh were America's golden couple, to such an extent that they felt compelled to flee from the public's admiring gaze. They built a house on a remote tract of land in New Jersey near the little town of Hopewell and here, on June 22, 1930, their first child was born.

"The Eaglet" as the child came to be known, lived for less than two years. On the cold, rainy night of May 1, 1932, somewhere between 8 and 10 pm, the little boy was kidnapped. Lindbergh was out hunting with his Springfield rifle for signs of the kidnapper when the State Police arrived, headed by their chief, H. Norman Schwarzkopf (father of "Stormin" Norman Schwarzkopf). Lindbergh had already found an envelope, but had not opened it. The police had no such qualms. Inside they found a ransom note in blue ink demanding $50,000. Details of where to place the money would follow. The police were not to be informed. Three days later another note arrived, raising the ransom to $70,000. Lindbergh was prepared to do whatever was asked for the return of his child. A further three days later, a certain John F. Condon offered his services as a go-between.

Condon was the first of many larger-than-life characters to become involved in the case. He was a windbag, a self-promoter and a bungler, but Lindbergh and the kidnapper accepted his services. A meeting was arranged at the Woodlawn Cemetery in the Bronx with a man who called himself "Cemetery John", following which the child's sleeping suit was mailed to Lindbergh. A second meeting was arranged, attended by both Condon and Lindbergh. They heard Cemetery John

Lindbergh Baby

Charles Augustus Lindbergh Jnr in happier days,
before he became the most famous baby in the world.

contained arsenic. Then Condon himself became a suspect. Schwarzkopf and his men tapped Condon's telephone, intercepted his mail, dug holes in his yard and even stripped the paper from the walls of his house, before deciding he was eccentric, but not guilty.

And then, almost a year after the discovery of the body, some of the ransom money turned up at a gas station in the Bronx. The gas station manager thought it odd that a customer should pay for 98 cents of gas with a $10 bill, and noted the licence plate number on the car. It turned out to be registered to a man named Bruno Hauptmann, a German who had entered the States illegally in 1923.

Hauptmann's trial, acerbically labelled "the greatest story since the Resurrection" by H. L. Mencken, was held in Fleming, New Jersey. Right to the end, the Crime of the Century threw up bizarre, oversize characters. The prosecuting Attorney General, David T. Wilenz, was a mixture of dandy and bully, after the style of Al Capone. The defence counsel, Edward J. Reilly, was a bully, a womanizer and a boozer, whose afternoon performances in court were remarkably listless. Two weeks after the verdict, Reilly was taken to a Brooklyn hospital in a straitjacket.

Hauptmann was found guilty. In the little time between sentence and execution, he was vilified in the press, but later doubts were voiced as to the justice of his trial and sentence. For 60 years, up to her death in 1994, his widow Anna persisted that he had been innocent. As for the Lindberghs, they had another son, and left the United States to settle in Europe, where the "Lone Eagle" sadly became a great admirer of Hermann Göring and the Luftwaffe.

call to them in a strong German accent. Lindbergh handed over $50,000 in "gold notes" and received a note allegedly telling him where to find the victim. It was now over a month since the little boy had been taken.

The note was worthless. Another month was to pass before the body of Charles Jnr was found, just six kilometres (four miles) from home. It was little more than a skeleton, hidden in a heap of rotting vegetation. The left leg, left hand and right arm were missing. The cause of death was a massive fracture of the skull. It was a shocking discovery.

At first, one of the Lindbergh's servants was suspected of the crime. The poor woman was so upset by such an accusation that she killed herself, swallowing silver polish that

(*top left*) Charles Lindbergh on the morning of the opening of Hauptmann's trial. (*left*) Bruno Hauptmann leaves New York Police Headquarters, September 21, 1934. (*top right*) Newspaper reporters and members of the public surround the spot where the Lindbergh baby's body was found, four miles from the Lindbergh home. (*right*) The handwriting evidence that did much to convict Hauptmann. The lower "signature" was constructed from letters taken from the ransom note.

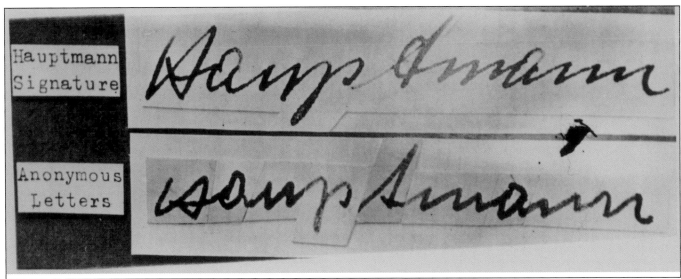

Hauptmann Signature

Anonymous Letters

On February 4, 1974, 19-year-old Patty Hearst was abducted from the apartment she shared with her partner in Berkeley, California. Her kidnappers were members of the Symbionese Liberation Army (SLA), an American para-military group with revolutionary ideals. Their aim was to hold her until other members of the SLA were released from prison. They had chosen Patty because she was the granddaughter of the newspaper tycoon, William Randolph Hearst. Negotiations for the exchange failed, however, and the SLA then demanded the distribution of $6 million worth of food among the poor of the Bay Area of California. The Hearst family complied with this request, but the SLA did not release Patty.

A few weeks later, however, Patty appeared in a new guise. On April 15 she was caught on a surveillance camera, wielding an assault rifle and participating in the robbery of the Sunset District branch of the Hibernia National Bank in San Francisco. Perhaps coincidentally, perhaps not, when Patty had attended the Santa Catalina School for Girls in Monterey, she had been friends with Patricia Tobin, whose family had founded the Hibernia National Bank. Following the robbery, Patty sent messages saying that she was now committed to the goals of the SLA.

In September 1975, she was arrested. Four months later, she was brought to trial. Her defence was that she had been physically and sexually abused by her captors, and also brainwashed so that she had no option but to join them. It was not a convincing defence and was poorly presented by her attorney, whom some allege was drunk during the trial. What happened may have been an extreme case of the "Stockholm syndrome", where captives identify with their captors. In any event, Patty Hearst was found guilty. Three years later, her sentence was commuted by President Jimmy Carter, and she was released in 1979. In January 2001, she was granted a full pardon by Bill Clinton on the last day of his Presidency.

Patty Hearst

The surveillance camera image of American heiress Patty Hearst taking part in a San Francisco bank robbery, April 15, 1974.

In 1977 a story broke that had tabloid reporters in Britain drooling. The story was: ex-Miss Wyoming fails to seduce pop star, joins Church of the Latter Day Saints, abducts young Mormon missionary, forces him to have kinky sex, is charged with kidnap, jumps bail and disappears. The ex-beauty queen was Joyce McKinney. The pop star, who showed good judgement in not falling for her charms, was Wayne Osmond. The poor abused Mormon was 21-year-old Kirk Anderson. Also involved was McKinney's partner in crime, Keith May. What gave the story even more zest was that while May was obsessed with McKinney, she cared not a jot for him, being obsessed with Anderson. It was a *ménage a trois* of spectacularly complicated proportions.

The press could not believe its luck. Here was a beautiful, intelligent and highly articulate woman prepared to tell all in a seductive Southern drawl that made what she said all the more exciting. And here was a victim who corroborated her story in fine detail. Anderson told those in the suburban courtroom at Epsom, Surrey, that he had been taken by May and McKinney to a lonely cottage, and tied to a bed with leather straps, padlocks, chains and ropes. "She grabbed my pyjamas and tore them from my body," he said. "She proceeded to have intercourse. I did not want it to happen. I was very upset."

McKinney endorsed Anderson's account. "Kirk has to be tied up to have an orgasm," she said. "The thought of being powerless before a woman seems to excite him." Later she made the strength of her own feelings perfectly clear. "I loved Kirk so much that I would have skied down Mount Everest in the nude with a carnation up my nose."

It never came to that. The trial was fixed for May 1978. By then McKinney had fled to the States, via Ireland and Canada, and in her absence, she was sentenced to a year's imprisonment. She never reappeared, leaving the press to dream and mourn "The Story That Got Away".

Joyce McKinney

In a police van taking her to court, a distraught Joyce McKinney holds up her version of what happened, November 23, 1977.

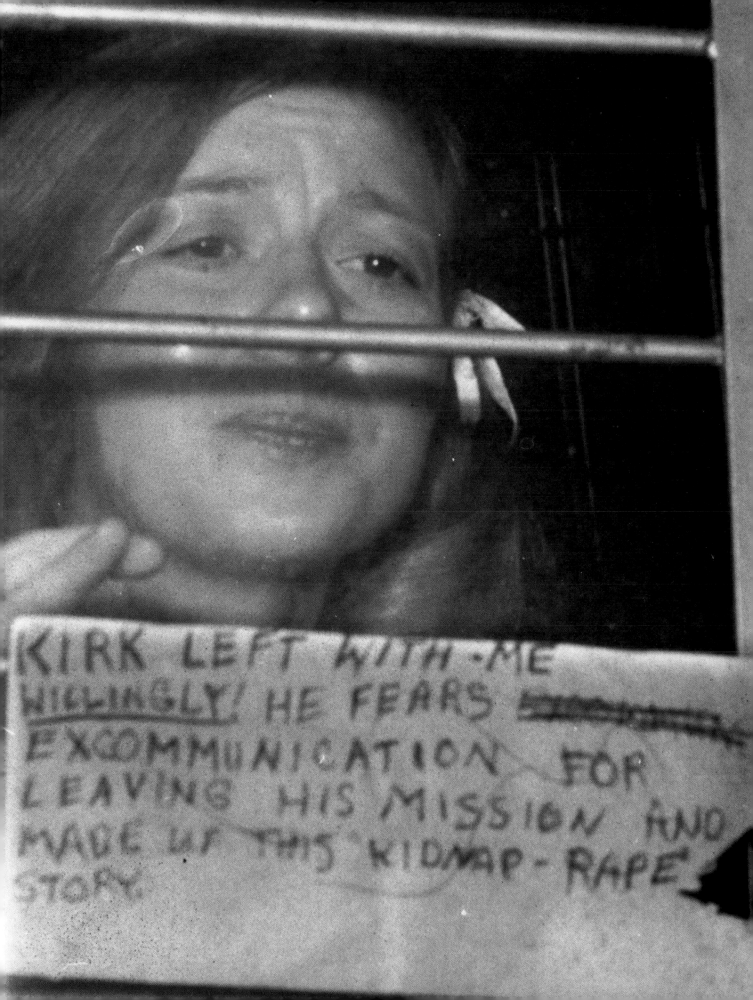

Aldo Moro's body was found in the boot of a car parked in the Via Caetani, Rome, on May 19, 1978. It was riddled with bullets. The car had been left, symbolically, halfway between the headquarters of the Italian Democrazia Cristiana (Christian Democrats) and the offices of the Italian Communist Party. During the last years of his life Moro – an ex-Prime Minister of Italy – had been working tirelessly to bring these parties together in what was known as the *Compromesso Storico* (Historic Compromise). Such a realignment would have brought a measure of political stability to Italy which some organizations did not want.

One such organization was the Red Brigade (RB), a left-wing terrorist unit formed in 1970 with the single aim of overthrowing capitalist Italy by violent means. Early in 1978, several leaders of the RB were imprisoned, and the RB was seeking a way of setting them free. So, on March 16, a group of Red Brigade commandos led by Mario Moretti kidnapped Moro, snatching him at gunpoint from his car during the morning rush hour. Five members of Moro's motorcycle escort were killed. It happened on a significant day, for Moro was on his way to the Italian House of Representatives to push forward the *Compromesso Storico*. The Red Brigade then issued a statement that they would free Moro only when their 14 colleagues were released from prison.

Much happened during the nine weeks between kidnap and killing. Moro was taken by his captors to a safe house, from which he was allowed to send letters to his family, fellow politicians and Pope Paul VI. Some of these letters were not published until almost 20 years later. Not surprisingly, in them Moro urged the government to come to terms with his kidnappers, but Italian political opinion was divided as to whether or not a deal should be struck with the Red Brigade. Some Christian Democrats denied the validity of such letters, claiming that they had been written under coercion. The government took a hard line stance – "the State must not bend" – though this was

Aldo Moro

A picture of Aldo Moro taken while he was held a prisoner in the Red Brigade "safe house", March 1978.

in sharp contrast to an earlier view when a politician named Ciro Cirillo had been kidnapped earlier. What is certain is that some members of both the Christian Democrats and the Communist Party objected to the *Compromesso* and did not wish to see Moro's safe return.

So the Red Brigade executed him. They put him in the boot of the car and told him to cover himself with a blanket. Ten bullets were fired into him, probably by Mario Moretti.

(*left*) The bullet-riddled body of Aldo Moro lies in the boot of the car parked in the Via Caetani, Rome. The case provoked a storm of protest and criticism of both the police and the government, and the choice of the Via Caetani was seen as a deliberate challenge to the Italian administration. (*above*) Crowds gather to mourn the death of the former Prime Minister of Italy.

On the afternoon of August 23, 2006, the citizens of Strasshof, Lower Austria, were confronted by a little girl begging them to call the police. Most took no notice, but an elderly woman realized something was wrong and made the call. The police arrived within 10 minutes.

The "little girl" was a young woman named Natascha Kampusch. She was 18 years old, and she had lived for eight years in a five square metre cellar beneath a garage, the steel door to which was hidden behind a cupboard. The cell was soundproof, windowless and, Natascha believed, booby-trapped. Her jailer, Wolfgang Priklopil, had told her that if she attempted to escape, she would be blown to pieces.

Priklopil had snatched Natascha on her way to school on March 2, 1998. After the first six months, he allowed her into the house, and gave her books to read. Later, he let her into the garden, strictly under his supervision. Natascha described herself as feeling "like a poor chicken in a hen house".

On the afternoon of her escape, she was vacuuming Priklopil's car when he received a call on his mobile phone. He walked away to take it, and Natascha fled. She had been imprisoned for 3,096 days, and had put on only three kilograms in weight and grown only 15 centimetres. As for Priklopil, he committed suicide the day Natascha escaped, throwing himself in front of a train near Vienna Northern Station.

Phillip Garrido was already on parole for a previous child kidnapping when he and his wife Nancy bundled 11-year-old Jaycee Lee Dugard into a grey sedan car in South Lake Tahoe, California, on June 10, 1991. The abduction was witnessed by her stepfather, and the search for Jaycee was immediate and widespread, although unsuccessful.

Stolen Childhood

A family photo of Jaycee Lee Dugard, taken a short while before her abduction by Phillip and Nancy Garrido. Like Natascha Kampusch, Jaycee had been waiting for the school bus when she was kidnapped.

Like Priklopil, Garrido had a prison prepared for his victim – his own backyard, an area surrounded by tall trees and a two-metre high fence, containing tents and outbuildings, an old car and a camping-style shower and toilet – more an open prison than a dungeon. For 18 years, Jaycee lived here, giving birth to two daughters (Angel and Starlit), probably fathered by her jailer.

Garrido was a sexual deviant, a chronic drug-abuser, and a self-styled evangelist. He took tremendous risks with his prisoner, allowing Jaycee to open the door to strangers, answer the phone and work as a designer in his print shop. Callers reported the presence of an unknown juvenile at the Garrido property, which constituted a violation of Garrido's parole from his previous kidnapping. Unhappily, local agencies failed to share this information, and there was no investigation.

Garrido's arrogance led him to go too far. On August 24, 2009, he took Jaycee and her two daughters to a meeting he had with his parole officer, who noted that the girls

(above) A video-screen image of Natascha Kampusch during her first television interview on Austrian television, September 6, 2006. Kampusch had been offered "vast sums" by the media for such an interview. Following her appearance, revelations of ineptitude in the investigation of her case from 1998 came to light.

called Garrido "Daddy" – Garrido reportedly had no children. He was arrested. Three days later, from his cell, Garrido told a TV reporter that he had a "powerful, heart-warming story to tell". Jaycee took her children home to her own mother. Garrido is still in prison.

Josef Fritzl was the father of all his prisoners. His appalling story began in 1977, when he first abused his daughter Elisabeth. The abuse continued for seven years, during

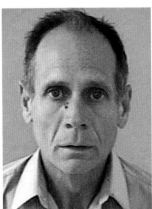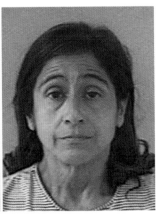

(*left*) Phillip and Nancy Garrido, shortly after their arrests in Placerville, California, August 27, 2009. (*above*) Tarps, tents, huts, and makeshift screens in the back-yard of Garrido's property in Antioch, California. This is where Jaycee Lee Dugard was held prisoner from June 1991 to August 2009.

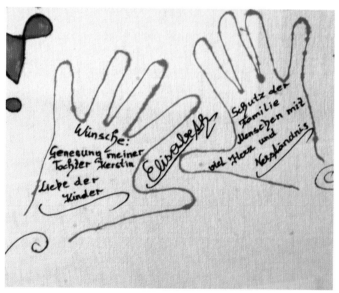

which Fritzl's wife Rosemarie apparently remained in total ignorance of what was happening. On August 29, 1984, he drugged the teenage Elisabeth, and locked her in an underground apartment he had purpose-built as her prison. Fritzl then told his wife that Elisabeth had run away from home.

Over the next 12 years, Fritzl fathered seven children with poor Elisabeth. One mercifully died. Of the others, Fritzl kept three underground with their mother, taking the other three upstairs and telling his wife that they were Elisabeth's babies, abandoned by her and left as foundlings on the doorstep. Rosemarie Fritzl accepted this explanation.

Every three days, Fritzl brought food and supplies to his underground family, sometimes sharing a meal and watching TV with them. While the children were in one room, Fritzl raped Elisabeth in another. He threatened to kill them if they tried to escape. Such an attempt would have failed, for the only two doors to the cellar weighed 500 kilograms and 300 kilograms respectively, far too heavy for his prisoners to shift.

The hideous state of affairs came to an end on April 19, 2008. Fritzl was forced to phone for an ambulance; his daughter Kerstin had collapsed with kidney failure. The terrible secret became world news, Fritzl was labelled a monster, a man who had committed crimes of unmatchable bestiality. At his trial, Fritzl claimed he had wanted to protect Elisabeth from the evils of the outside world, and that as a child he had been ill-treated by his mother after his father had abandoned them. The court, the media and the public rejected these admittedly unhappy experiences as an excuse for what he had done. Fritzl was sentenced to life imprisonment.

(top) Josef Fritzl on the fourth day of his trial at Saint Poelten, Austria, March 19, 2009. (above) Detail from a poster made by Fritzl's family and displayed in a shop window in Amstetten, May 14, 2008. The text reads: "We, the whole family, want to take this opportunity to thank you all for your sympathies with our fate. Your compassion helps us to cope with this difficult time and shows us that there are also good and honest people. We hope the time will come for us to regain normal life." (opposite) A sign on the fence outside Fritzl's house reads: "Why didn't anybody notice?"

Index

Picture Acknowledgements

Even with 70 million images to choose from amongst the vast archives and collections of Getty Images the editors' task for this project was daunting. Much thanks go to our colleagues at Agence France Presse, to Jeff Burak and Michelle Franklin at Time & Life Pictures, and to Mitch Blank and Kristeen Ballard at Getty Images in New York.

The Editors also wish to thank Topham Picturepoint for supplying the picture on page 187. All other pictures are courtesy of the various collections either held or represented by Getty Images. Those requiring further attribution are indicated as follows:

Key
t top **m** middle **b** bottom **l** left **r** right **i** inset

AFP Agence France Presse **AS** American Stock **CNP** Consolidated News Pictures **LOC** Library of Congress **NA** National Archives **NYT** New York Times Co. **T&LP** Time & Life Pictures

2 Vernon Merritt III/T&LP; **8-9, 12tr, 12bl** AS; **13t** LOC #3a50864; **14t** John Swartz/AS; **18-19** AS; **21** Mansell/T&LP; **27br, 29** AS; **31t, 35t** AFP; **35b** T&LP; **36-7** Francis Miller/T&LP; **46b** Dennis Oulds; **49tl** Paul S Howell; **49tr** Dave Einsel; **49bl** Pam Francis; **49br** James Nielsen/AFP; **51** Franck Prevel; **54-5** Ian Cook/T&LP; **59** Davis; **67** Terry Fincher; **68tl** Mitchell; **75** Ralph Crane/T&LP; **76t** State of Mississippi Attorney General's Office; **76b** Kyle Carter; **77** NA; **79** Terry Smith/T&LP; **81** LAPD; **82t** Jean-Marc Giboux; **82b** LAPD/AFP; **83t** AFP; **83b** Richard Creamer; **84** Vince Bucci/AFP; **85** AFP; **86-7** David Lees/T&LP; **89** T&LP; **93, 97** Hank Walker/T&LP; **100t** Slim Aarons; **103** AS; **109, 111b, 112b** Fotos International; **110-11** Vernon Merritt III/T&LP; **112tl** Terry O'Neill; **112tr** Ralph Crane/T&LP; **113** Julian Wasser/T&LP; **115** David Hume Kennerly; **117** Tim Roberts/AFP; **118l** Bob Daemmrich/AFP; **118-19** Jim Bourg; **121** Dimitar Dilkoff/AFP; **122** Jerry Lampen/AFP; **123** Savo Prelevic/AFP; **125, 126bl, br** Jefferson County Sheriff's Department; **126tl** T&LP; **126-7** Mark Leffingwell/AFP; **128-9** Scott Peterson; **131** FBI; **132** Bob Houlihan/US Navy; **133** Peter C Brandt; **134** Mario Tama; **135** Stan Honda/AFP; **137** Christophe Simon/AFP; **157** Ralph Morse/T&LP; **159** AFP; **165, 168tmr, 169tr** Francis Miller/T&LP; **166-69** (all except **168tmr, 169tr**) Frank Scherschel/T&LP; **172-3** William H Alden; **176t, 177** Adrian Moreland; **176b** Jack Hickes; **179** Paul Hawthorne; **185-87** Terry Smith/T&LP; **189** Eugene Garcia/AFP; **190-1** Taro Yamasaki/T&LP; **193** EPA/PA/AFP; **194-5** Ian Cook/T&LP; **197** Greater Manchester Police; **200-1** Makaram Gad Alkareem/AFP; **204l** LOC #3a53289; **204r** LOC 3g05341; **205t** LOC #02961; **205b (l-r)** LOC #04208, #3g06468, #04213, #04221, #04217, #04218; **206-7** LOC #04230; **209** Austrian State Archives/Imagno; **212t, br** Mansell/T&LP; **217** Bilderwelt/Roger Viollet; **222** Art Rickerby/T&LP; **223t** Carl Mydans/T&LP; **223b** CBS Photo Archive; **224t** NA; **224b** T&LP; **225** Shel Hershorn/T&LP; **228b** Santi Visalli Inc.; **229t** Joseph Louw/T&LP; **229b** Henry Groskinsky/T&LP; **231** Bill Eppridge/T&LP; **233** Luiz Alberto; **235** AFP; **236tl** Michael Evans/CNP; **236bl** Dirck Halstead; **239** AFP; **240-1** Weegee (Arthur Fellig)/International Centre of Photography; **253** Thomas D McAvoy/T&LP; **260-1** Ed Lallo/T&LP; **271** Nat Farbman/T&LP; **275** Terry O'Neill; **276tl** George Cordell; **276tr** Aubrey Hart; **279** T&LP; **280-1** Mickey Pfleger/T&LP; **289** CNP; **291** Frank Barratt; **295tr** Hans Paul/AFP; **297** Mark Ralston/AFP; **298** AFP; **301** John MacDougall/AFP